a socialist world is possible
with new introduction

the history of the CWI by peter taaffe

CW00821451

a socialist world is possible

with new introduction

the history of the CWI by peter taaffe

published by CWI Publications & Socialist Books

August 2004

A Socialist World is Possible
The History of the CWI
by Peter Taaffe
© CWI Publications & Socialist Books 2004

First Edition August 2004

ISBN 1-870958 29 2 pbk

Published by CWI Publications and Socialist Books
for the Committee for a Workers International
Designed and typeset by Kavita Graphics
Typeset in Utopia 9 pt
Printed by Russell Press (Nottingham)

Distribution by Socialist Books
PO Box 24697, London, E11 1YD
Telephone +44 (0)20 8988 8777

typesetting & design: dennis@kavitagraphics.co.uk

a socialist world is possible
with new introduction

the history of the CWI by peter taaffe

History of the CWI
Introduction on the
30th anniversary

The thirtieth anniversary of the founding of the Committee for a Workers' International (CWI) took place in April 2004. The International Secretariat (IS) of the CWI decided to celebrate the activity and contribution of the CWI to the workers' movement internationally over the last 30 years by republishing an amended version of the pamphlet, 'History of the CWI', first written in 1997. The period since then has, however, been full of important events, incidents and developments – both objectively, and in the workers' movement. The role and influence of the CWI has developed but also changed, and in some regions and countries quite dramatically.

We have seen the emergence of the anti-capitalist movement, as well as the colossal elemental movement of millions in opposition to Bush and Blair's war in Iraq. This has been accompanied by a ferocious defensive struggle by the working class, particularly in Europe, against the brutal neo-liberal offensive launched by the capitalists against their rights and conditions. This has resulted in a series of strikes – some of them one-day general or public sector strikes – throughout the continent.

In view of this, the IS of the CWI felt that it was necessary to provide an update of the views of the CWI, both in relation to these developments and on how our role contrasts with the views and actions of others claiming to be Marxist or Trotskyist. Of necessity, this will involve an analysis of the policies and programme of other organisations and how they compare with those of the CWI. This method of making contrasts was employed by the great Marxists – beginning with Marx, as well as Engels, Lenin and Trotsky – when dealing with ideas, trends and organisations which they believed did not meet up to the needs of the working class and labour movement.

It has to be recognised that this method – polemics – fell somewhat out of fashion in the "post-modernist" period, particularly in the 1990s. "Conversations" – polite exchanges which passed as "debates" – became the norm for the ideologists of capitalism and their echoes, the leaders of the ex-social democratic and communist parties. The superiority of capitalism and the triumph of the "market" were to be automatically accepted; discussions were intended to take place within this context.

The sharpening of the political situation, however, particularly in the first few years of this new century, has resulted in more intense conflicts than was the norm in the 1990s. For instance, over the Iraq war there have been divisions even between the ruling circles of the US and Britain on the one side, and France and Germany on the other. Similarly, the embittered mood of the working class at the betrayals of right-wing labour and trade union leaders has resulted in angry demands within the labour movement for a lead to be given from the top and a clearer class explanation of the way forward. As always, the precondition for understanding what methods and organisation the working class needs in this era is organically linked to the understanding of the main political features of the situation. This, in turn, involves understanding recent history and how changes, some of them extremely sharp in character, have taken place or will take place in the next period.

The situation in the 1990s proved to be difficult terrain for the CWI and others who stood on the left, particularly the socialist and Marxist-Trotskyist left. The collapse of Stalinism ushered in an entirely different period to that which had confronted previous generations in the 20th Century; it was the most difficult, in a sense, for 50 years. No other Trotskyist 'International' understood so quickly and clearly the main features of the situation which flowed from the collapse of the Berlin Wall as the CWI. With the Berlin Wall collapsed not just Stalinism but also the planned economies of Eastern Europe and the Soviet Union.

In contrast, as we shall see from an analysis of the positions of different organisations, some acted like political ostriches. They buried their heads in the sand, refusing to recognise until much later that these events represented a major defeat for the workers' movement internationally. Some saw it as a 'setback' but not of a decisive character. Others viewed it as a terrible historical catastrophe; socialism and the prospects for a socialist revolution were off the agenda for decades, if not for ever. The CWI concluded that the collapse of Stalinism was a defeat and a serious one, but not on the scale of those of the interwar period, when fascist regimes triumphed in Italy, Germany and Spain. These had prepared the way for the calamity of the Second World War and its countless victims.

The collapse of Stalinism did provide world capitalism with the possibility of indicting 'socialism' as an 'historic failure' (it falsely equated socialism with the Stalinist regimes). This, in turn, provided them with the opportunity to conduct a ferocious ideological campaign against the ideas of socialism. At the same time, they argued from a thousand platforms that only the 'market' could provide a permanent model for humankind. This was summed up by Frances Fukiyama's 'sophisticated' assertion that "History has ended". By this, he meant that liberal, capitalist democracy could not be improved upon. It was, therefore, the only form of organisation of society which was now possible or desirable.

Greenspan declares triumph of "market economies"

The Wall Street Journal, more crudely, simply declared on behalf of the big business jackals that it represented, and world capitalism as a whole: "We won!" Even recently, the spokespersons of US imperialism – seeking reassurance for themselves and their class in a more troubled world than appeared likely in the post-1989 situation – extolled the virtues of their system and made the same point. Alan Greenspan, chairman of the US Federal Reserve Bank, and chief economic guru for US capitalism, recently declared when in Berlin: "I have maintained over the years that the most profoundly important debate between conflicting theories of optimum economic organisation during the twentieth century was settled, presumably definitively, here more than a decade ago in the aftermath of the dismantling of the Berlin Wall. Aside from the Soviet Union itself, the economies of the Soviet bloc had been, in the pre-war period, similar in many relevant respects to the market-based economies of the west. Over the first four decades of post-war Europe, both types of economies developed side by side with limited interaction. It was as close to a controlled experiment in the viability of economic systems as could ever be implemented.

"The results, evident with the dismantling of the Wall, were unequivocally in favour of market economies. The consequences were far-reaching. The long-standing debate between the virtues of economies organised around free markets and those governed by centrally planned socialism, one must assume, is essentially at an end. To be sure, a few still support an old-fashioned socialism. But for the vast majority of previous adherents it is now a highly diluted socialism, an amalgam of social equity and market efficiency, often called market socialism. The verdict on rigid central planning has been rendered, and it is generally appreciated to have been unqualifiedly negative. There was no eulogy for central planning; it just ceased to be mentioned, and a large majority of developing nations quietly shifted from socialism to more market-oriented economies.".[1]

However, against the background of a looming world economic meltdown and the catastrophic chaos in the wake of the invasion and occupation of Iraq, these comments by Greenspan amount to little more than whistling in the dark to keep up the spirits of the possessing classes that he represents. His remarks pertain to the previous era of the 1990s. For a while in the 1990s, socialist consciousness – and the broad understanding of the working class, in particular – was undoubtedly thrown back. Weakened though it was, the basic potential power of the working class remained intact. The relationship of class forces was not as significantly weighted in favour of the ruling class as it was in the 1930s.

The ideological campaign of the bourgeois undoubtedly had a material effect in underpinning neo-liberal policies, which weakened the rights and conditions of the working class. The other side of the coin, however, is that intensified capitalist global-isation has lowered national barriers, certainly as far as the 'free movement of capital' is concerned. It has led to the rapid transfer of resources from one country and one continent to another. All this has compelled working class people into thinking in continental and even world terms. In other words, capitalism has prepared the objective basis for a new internationalism in outlook, manifested, in the first instance, in the powerful 'anti-capitalist globalisation' movements of the late 1990s and the early part of this century.

From London to Seattle, from Prague to the historic and bloody clashes in Genoa and Gothenburg, at Nice, Quebec, Porto Allegre, Paris and Mumbai, inhumane, 'modern' capitalism, and its brutal juggernaut of globalisation, were rejected. In the first instance, this has been manifested in the changes in outlook and the actions of young people, supported, in some instances, by significant sections of workers. In the germ, this is a new internationalism that identifies with the struggle of the 'people' in continental and global terms. However, a class differentiation will come at a certain stage. Karl Marx was the first to recognise "globalisation" in his day, the development of a world market, and with it, the world working class, which made possible 'world history': "The proletariat can…only exist *world-historically*, just as communism, its movement, can only have a 'world-historical' existence."[2] And further: "The extension of markets into a world-market, which has now become possible and was daily becoming more and more a fact, called forth a new phase of historical development…".[3]

This was at a time when the interdependence of the world, through the develop-ment of a world division of labour, was in its "infancy", compared to today and largely invisible to the mass of the population.

Big movements of peoples

How different the situation is today. Through the internet, worldwide satellite television and its 24-hour news, foreign travel, etc., the binding together of the world is a palpable and visible reality recognised by the majority of the world's population! Television and even mobile phones are increasingly available in some of the most economically underdeveloped and deprived regions of the planet. This is a manifestation of Marx's law of "combined and uneven development"; the latest word in technique is battened on to feudal and semi-feudal social relations. Technology is employed in economically underdeveloped societies which have yet to complete the "bourgeois-democratic, national and democratic revolution". Involving a thoroughgoing land reform, unification of the country and the develop-ment of these societies along modern lines, this revolution was carried out by the capitalists in Europe hundreds of years ago. However, in large parts of Asia, Africa and even in Latin America, the bourgeois-democratic revolution can only be carried through by the working class coming to power and mobilising the rural population behind them, thereby establishing workers' power – a workers and peasants' government. This in turn would entail going over to socialist measures, on a national, continental and world scale. This is the essence of Trotsky's 'Theory of the Permanent Revolution'. It retains its full validity today in those countries which are kept in backwardness and poverty by capitalism through the perpetuation of feudal, semi-feudal, and archaic social and economic relations.

But humankind does not stand still and is not acquiescent in the face of stagnant or deteriorating conditions. Worldwide means of communication put on view a better life for some in the world when set against the grinding poverty of the majority. It produces a magnet for the most energetic section of the population in Africa, Asia and Latin America, or those with resources, to seek access to the advanced goods and higher living standards in Europe, in Japan and the US. There have been big movements of people, migrating from deprived areas by taking any opportunity to escape or they have been driven from their homes by wars or persecution.

The reaction of the capitalists to this is shot through with hypocrisy and contradictions. They are forced to depend on immigrants to fill low-paid sweated jobs, as well as trying to plug the "skills gap". Through the influx of younger immigrants, they are also attempting to compensate for the aging of their populations. At the same time, the capitalists still seek to use immigrants as scapegoats for the ills of their system. Talking of "Fortress Europe" is also an attempt to outflank the European far right, who threaten the electoral position of the main capitalist parties.

However, while immigrants beat a path to the doors of the advanced industrial societies, an opposite process is taking place – a massive 'relocation' of jobs, both in manufacturing and in recently created 'service' occupations – to China, India and other parts of the 'underdeveloped' world. This now includes Eastern Europe, if not Russia, as well. This poses sharply on a national scale the need for a programme for workers, particularly the trade unions, to defend their jobs against this pernicious 'outsourcing', as well as defending the union rights of immigrant workers. This is merely the latest manifestation of the ingrained drive of the capitalists to 'maximise' their profits. If this be at the cost of the loss of millions of relatively high-paid jobs in the manufacturing sector replaced, they reason, in some cases only partially, by temporary lower-paid jobs in the so-called 'service' industries - then so be it! To take one example of the fate of workers in 'modern' capitalism; one third of the Spanish labour force is on temporary contracts with an average time span of ten days!

The consequence of this is the impoverishment of significant sections of the working class. Formerly high-paid, securely employed workers with hard-won rights have been replaced by a new army of the poor –not just unemployed but 'working poor'. This is creating the conditions for a massive revolt of low-paid, impoverished sections of the working class. It could develop along the lines of the uprising of the gas workers, dockers and match workers, in Britain, during the late nineteenth century. This was paralleled by similar movements, at different stages in history, in other countries in Europe and in the US. The argument of the 'high priests' of capitalism is that the process of globalisation is inexorable. It cannot be stopped. Moreover, it will ultimately benefit everyone by creating new jobs in new industries, both in the neo-colonial world and in the industrialised (now becoming de-industrialised) sectors of the world economy.

Tell that to the women workers in the maquiladores in Mexico, where the venal bosses prefer female labour, usually single mothers, because they are the least able to resist through strike action the onslaught of capital's drive to cut wages and conditions. The proponents of the North American Free Trade Agreement (NAFTA) – between the US, Canada and Mexico – argued that the Agreement would be for the mutual benefit of the working class in both North and Central America. Instead, millions of US jobs were relocated to Mexico, while the conditions of the working class in Mexico, allegedly 'benefiting' from these jobs, actually deteriorated.

From their experiences, the idea will ineluctably grow within the ranks of the working class that the employers should not be allowed to close factories like a child closing a matchbox or move productive facilities from one country or continent to another without resistance.

The need for a common policy of workers in different countries – for instance, in Europe, in the next period – co-ordinated through the trade unions for common rates, will take root amongst workers. The same process will develop in relation to workers in China, India and elsewhere. Already they are ferociously resisting the newly-arrived venal capitalism that wishes to super-exploit them and their families. This new internationalism on an industrial plane is paralleled on the political terrain. Efforts are being made, fumbling and faltering as they are, to seek to link up international, continental and world political resistance. Utopian though they are, even proposals like that of the British environmentalist writer George Monbiot to establish a 'world parliament' (outlined in his book 'Age of Consent') to check and control capitalism, are manifestations of the demands arising within the anticapitalist movement for international, political solutions to the problems which exist now.

This process has been furthered by the increased awareness of the colossal polarisation of wealth, both within and between nations, which has developed in the 1990s. The ten richest people on earth possessed, in 2002, a combined wealth of $266 billion. This is five times the annual flow of aid from rich nations to poor ones. It is roughly sufficient to pay for all the United Nations' "millennium goals", such as halting and reversing the spread of AIDS, malaria and other infectious diseases, reducing infant mortality by two-thirds and lowering the number of maternal deaths in childbirth by three-quarters between now and 2050.

The statistics that demonstrate the scale and depth of world poverty are well rehearsed. Big parts of the world's population are now conscious that half of the globe lives on $2 a day or less, and one-fifth on less than $1 a day. Despite a global surplus of food, 840 million people are officially classified as malnourished, as they lack the money required to buy sufficient food. One hundred and eighty-four million people are unemployed throughout the world (and this excludes the 'underemployed'). The World Bank has estimated that 54 countries, with a combined population of 750 million people, have actually seen deterioration in their real incomes in the past 10 years.

The real power on the planet is vested in 500 individuals (predominantly rich men and with only a few women). They control the majority of the means of production – the organisation of labour, science, technique, etc. The institutions of world capitalism – the World Bank, International Monetary Fund, buttressed by military alliances such as NATO – are subordinate ultimately to this power, which is reflected through the so-called 'hidden hand' of the market. National governments seem powerless against 'investors' who, in the new deregulated global capitalism, can bring governments to their knees unless they come to heel like obedient dogs. The Clinton presidency in the United States was forced by the pressure of the market, particularly the buyers of government debt, to abandon its tepid stimulus programme in 1993. Clinton turned himself into an "Eisenhower Republican". This was in order to satisfy what the former president called "a bunch of fucking bond traders".[4]

First stages of global revolt

The movement against capitalist globalisation represents the first stages of this international revolt against the world capitalist system. Its great merit is that it has mobilised millions of people, particularly young people, into action for the first time. Not all of those participating in the movement consciously opposed capitalism; they were initially in revolt against the effects of capitalism on living standards, the environment, increased militarisation, the drive to war and the monstrous future which this system has conjured up for humankind.

Up to now, where the labour movement and the working class have participated in the anti-capitalist movement, it has usually been in a subordinate position, not coming out as an independent force or with its own political banners. This is largely because of the role of the right-wing trade union leaders, supported, of course, by the leaders of the ex-workers' parties in Europe and elsewhere, who are now bulwarks of world capitalism. Nevertheless, it is not possible to overestimate this movement, in its scope as an anticipation of future mass movements of the working class. A mass movement of the workers will be more conscious of capitalism being the barrier to further progress and will instinctively pose class demands as a solution to the problems of the world.

The anti-capitalist movement has concentrated on opposition to many of the institutions of world capitalism, such as the IMF and World Bank. This flows from the policy of many of the leaders of the movement. They do not believe it is possible to direct a frontal attack on capitalism and, therefore, wish to channel it merely into a critique of aspects of modern capitalism. Some, like George Monbiot, are searing in their criticisms of the World Bank, the IMF and even the United Nations. Monbiot also shows in detail the futility of imagining that serious "reforms" of these institutions are possible, as some others in the anticapitalist movement have suggested. But having gone far in his criticism, Monbiot draws back and, in effect, seeks solutions within the confines of the system.

The millions-fold movement from below, however, is crossing over the threshold which Monbiot and other leaders of the movement baulk at. In the future it will go much further. Its activists are searching for a programme and ideas which can create a real alternative "new world". This cannot be a renovated capitalist programme but must be socialist in content. The mass movement against the war in Iraq has resulted in a profound change in consciousness of all layers in society but particularly amongst young people. Marxists have always pointed out that war is the midwife of revolution. For instance, the 1905 Russian Revolution was ushered in by the Russo-Japanese War and the 1917 Russian Revolution by the First World War. The Iraq War has not yet led to a revolution, apart from the mass resistance in Iraq to occupation, which is potentially the beginning of a revolution. But it has led to a revolution, or the beginning of revolution, in the outlook of millions who have been radicalised by these convulsive events. In the minds of many, the need for an alternative has been posed, with some embracing socialism.

How to realise this "new world" demanded by increasing sections of the movement is a key question. History, including recent history, has shown that this will not be achieved either 'spontaneously' or 'semi-spontaneously'. The twentieth century was marked by heroic movements of the working class, revolutionary upsurges, which reached out to take power from the capitalists. In some cases power slipped from the hands of the working class. This was the case in Spain, 1936-37, where initially four-fifths of the country was under the control of the working class. In Chile, under Allende in 1973, 40 per cent of land and industry was taken out of private hands, while in Portugal, in 1975, a mass movement from below compelled the government to nationalise the banks and, through them, 70 per cent of industry. The failure of the working class to hold onto power arose not at all from its political 'immaturity', but entirely because their own organisations, in particular, their leaders, at the head of mass socialist and communist parties, proved a barrier. In almost every case these leaders handed power back to the capitalists, rather than seek a solution to the workers' needs and demands through revolution.

The 'Internationals'

All these movements were instinctively internationalist – looking for solutions on the international plane – and evoked tremendous support from the world working class as a consequence.

From its inception as a force in its own right, the working class looked for a solution not just on the national sphere but internationally, as well. The Communist League was organised by the young Marx and Engels in the 1840s when the influence of Chartism in Britain – the first independent industrial and political movement of the working class worldwide – was still felt. Indeed, there have been five serious attempts to harness the mass political power of the working class on a world scale: the Communist League, The International Working Men's Association, also organised by Marx and Engels, the Socialist (Second) International, the Communist (Third) International, following the Russian Revolution, and Trotsky's Fourth International. All of these organisations played an important role in raising and enhancing the power and understanding of the working class, as we have explained in the History of the CWI.

Yet, in this first decade of the twenty-first century, when capitalism demonstrates its failures and, at the same time, globalisation enhances the case for real internationalism and an international organisation, there is no mass political international of the working class based on mass parties. The task of the CWI is to help to create the conditions for the formation of such an International. However, this is only possible on the basis of learning from the lessons from the past and, particularly, from the failings of previous Internationals. A big step towards such a mass International would be the creation of mass parties on a national level. But the outline of such an International cannot be left until the creation of such parties. A powerful embryo for a mass International must be created in the new explosive period that is opening up. We believe the CWI can play a vital role in this process.

However, the political terrain is littered with the remnants of failed and would-be 'Internationals'. Some of them had very shallow roots in the real movement of the working class, if any at all. Most of these organisations are fragments. Most are either organically opportunist or ultra-left; many of them, unfortunately, stand under the banner of 'Trotskyism'. We explained in the 1997 of the 'History of the CWI' the reasons why Trotsky's original conception of the 'Fourth International', launched in 1938, did not take off. It never became a mass force, although in some cases Trotskyism had a powerful effect on the labour movement, such as in Sri Lanka, Latin America, Vietnam, France, and Britain in the 1970s and 1980s. The reason why the 'Fourth International' did not succeed was because of a combination of unfavourable objective factors and difficulties, together with the mistakes made by the leaders of the 'Fourth International'.

The twenty-first century, however, presents an opportunity to learn from the past. The process can begin – some steps at least can be taken – to lay the foundations for such a new International. But this task is, first and foremost, political. The only justification for trying to build a political organisation, separate and apart from others, certainly as far as Marxists are concerned, is the existence of serious differences on policy and programme. Incidental, secondary, personal or tactical differences are not sufficient justification for maintaining a different organisation, particularly when such an organisation is numbered in dozens, hundreds or even thousands.

For this reason, following the collapse in the Berlin Wall and the new situation which opened up, the CWI did explore the possibility of whether we could arrive at agreement on fundamental issues with other trends within Trotskyism. We discussed and corresponded with the United Secretariat of the Fourth International (USFI, sometimes known as the Fourth International). We had connections and discussions with the Trotskyists around the 'Morenoite' current, largely based in Latin America. We sought to work, and still do (unfortunately with little success) in common organisations and alliances with the International Socialist Tendency (IST), whose most prominent section is the Socialist Workers Party (SWP) in Britain. We approached these discussions with an open mind in the hope that, as we had done, these organisations would perhaps learn from their past mistakes, readjust their political stance and, thereby, lay the basis for common work and possible political agreement on the tasks ahead.

Unfortunately, the conclusions which most of these organisations drew from the new world situation confronting the working class and the Marxist movement were at variance with ours, and in some cases quite decisively so. The collapse of Stalinism, symbolised in the fall of the Berlin Wall, was one of those decisive moments in history which, unless correctly assessed, can lead to grave mistakes, in policy, programme and organisation. None of these other organisations adjusted to the main features of the immediate post-Stalinist situation as quickly or as clearly as the CWI.

Scottish Socialist Party

The 'terrible nineties' that followed the collapse of Stalinism, is the objective source of the opportunism of many organisations. Paradoxically, developments within the CWI – the movement away from a revolutionary Trotskyist position by the leaders of what was to become the Scottish Socialist Party – inadvertently encouraged this process. The formation and electoral success of the Scottish Socialist Party (SSP) has now become a model for some of those who are in headlong retreat from Marxism and Trotskyism. The decision of the then leadership of the CWI section in

Scotland, in the late 1990s, to set up a broad socialist formation, the SSP, while effectively abandoning the revolutionary party, represented a fundamental break with the revolutionary programme, tactics and strategy of the CWI. This development, led by individuals who had played an important role in the CWI in the past, such as Tommy Sheridan, Alan McCombes and others, was not at all accidental. It was the product of the difficulties of continuing to argue for a revolutionary programme and approach in a dramatically changed political climate.

The proposals of these comrades, at the outset, did not appear to many as representing a fundamental departure from our analysis and programme. After all, it was the leadership of the CWI not the leadership of the Scottish section, Tommy Sheridan and Alan McCombes, who initially called for a new mass workers' party. This was based upon our analysis about the 'bourgeoisification' of the social democracy in Britain (New Labour) and, ultimately, social democracy worldwide. Despite the attempts of Alan McCombes and Tommy Sheridan to try and picture the CWI majority as rejecting the idea of forming a broad party, such arguments cut no ice with the majority of the CWI membership.

Our objection was to their liquidation of the revolutionary current within such a formation. The arguments in and around these ideas can be thoroughly examined by visiting the CWI website at *www.marxist.net*. The leadership of the CWI, with an overwhelming majority of the CWI behind it in the debate over this issue, correctly foretold the political evolution of what later became the leadership of the SSP. Despite their denials that this was their aim, we predicted their political backsliding and their ultimate liquidation into the SSP. This involved a shift towards reformism that, in practice, amounted to the winding up of Scottish Militant Labour, which had been a revolutionary party. To begin with, when Tommy Sheridan and Alan McCombes formed the International Socialist Movement within the SSP, this was not obvious. However, in January 2003, the leadership proposed winding up as the ISM, as the SSP was "doing the job". The proposal was put on ice until after the Scottish parliamentary elections that year. In October of the same year, it was raised again. It was agreed to maintain the ISM but there was little enthusiasm to build it. They needed to retain the semblance of an organisation because of political opposition within the ISM, as well as because of the danger which would then be presented to their position by other platforms within the SSP, particularly the CWI. The reality is that the ISM is the faction of the majority of the SSP leadership.

Despite this, the SSP has partially filled the vacuum which exists to the left of Labour and has had a measure of success electorally, as well as growing in numbers. Its electoral success in the 2003 Scottish parliamentary elections raised its profile further, as has the affiliation of the Scottish Rail, Maritime and Transport Union (RMT) branches to the SSP. As a result, in some quarters of the 'revolutionary left' internationally, this has been invoked as a model of how to lay the foundations for new parties of the working class. Heavy emphasis is laid on the need to go 'broad', involving, in practice, the submerging of revolutionary organisations into such formations. This seems to be justified by the success of the SSP. However, what is forgotten in all of this are the limits to what has been achieved in Scotland. Concrete, specific conditions exist there and, with different conditions elsewhere, it may not be possible to immediately reproduce an SSP-type party. Undoubtedly, the national question has given a sharpness to the political situation in Scotland, from which the SSP has benefited. However, the Socialist Party in England and Wales also has a credible record on the electoral field. The SP successfully stood in eleven elections at local level, leading to the election of socialist councillors and their re-election. Since 2001, the votes won in Coventry, during election campaigns for the Socialist Party's Dave Nellist, have been consistently the best of parties to the left of New Labour in England and Wales. Moreover, while the SSP polled a credible 5.2% of the vote in Scotland during the 2004 Euro elections, the SP (CWI) in Ireland won 5.5% across Dublin in the same EU poll. These election results underline the fact that electoral support can be won without abandoning a consistent Marxist and Trotskyist programme.

We welcomed and supported the setting up of the SSP – despite the completely false claims of the leadership of that party that we were opposed (for more details, see *www.marxist.net*). But we insisted on continuing with the maintenance and building of a clearly-identified Marxist trend within the SSP. This corresponds with the tactic set out in the 1990s – the dual task of fighting for and rehabilitating the basic ideas of socialism and, at the same time, building new parties of the working class while maintaining the ideas of revolutionary Marxism within these new organisations.

The SSP leadership subscribed to the first task but have abandoned the second, and vital, task for Marxists in this era. Through impatience – a drive for short-term popularity – they have watered down the ideas they formerly adhered to when in the CWI. Now neither they or we, nor any other serious organisation in the international movement today, would describe the SSP leaders as consistently 'Trotskyist'. They seek to put as much distance as possible between their present position and their revolutionary past in Militant and Scottish Militant Labour, as well as in the CWI.

Abandonment of Marxist position

The speeches of Tommy Sheridan are not consistently socialist and Marxist in content. For instance, as the convenor of the SSP, he explained in an interview on the BBC that, "there are a number of countries which have a successful mix of public ownership and high taxation... like Norway and Denmark they manage to combine high levels of public ownership with high taxation for the wealthy."

This implied that capitalist Norway and Denmark were the benchmark for the kind of Scotland that Tommy Sheridan wanted to see. He then went on to state: "I don't think there's a need to nationalise Tesco right now. What I think there's a need for is to impose on Tesco proper wages and employment conditions. What we would be doing is regulating business. You don't have to own it, you just regulate it." ('The Herald', Glasgow, 30 April 2003).

In the same interview Tommy Sheridan said: "What we're saying is that in a future independent, socialist Scotland, we want to work on training, on skills. We want to offer a very high-skilled economy, a motivated workforce for big business. If that can work in Germany and France, where they have higher wages, better standards and produce better products, why can't that work here in Scotland?"

Leaving aside Tommy Sheridan's wish to offer the big bosses a "highly motivated workforce", workers in Germany, some on 2 or 3 Euros an hour, and French workers, who see their pay and conditions under attack from Prime Minister Raffarin's neo-liberal programme, do not consider that they are "high paid"! Moreover, on a capitalist basis, "high wages" are becoming a thing of the past, in Germany and elsewhere.

In the SSP newspaper, 'The Voice', Kevin Williamson, a close collaborator of Tommy Sheridan and Alan McCombes, puts a non-class 'liberal' position (without any comment by them): "Those who see politics purely in terms of either capitalism or socialism have yet to make any serious attempt to explain how a controlling class can be prevented from arising to a position of power in a post-capitalist society. The rest of us need to put forward practical alternatives."

The same kind of retreat – compared to when they were in the CWI – applies to the SSP's stand on international issues. This goes from uncritical support of the Cuban state of Castro, which they describe as "socialist", to a complete abandonment of the socialist solution to the Palestinian-Israeli conflict – of a socialist Palestine and a socialist Israel within the framework of a socialist confederation of the Middle East. In effect, at the 2002 SSP conference, they accepted the Socialist Workers' Party's false slogan of 'a Palestinian state with minority rights for the Israelis'. Although at a subsequent conference this position was watered down, nevertheless, in the SSP newspapers and the public statements of leading SSP members, the idea of a Palestinian state with minority rights for Israelis still appears. Such an abstract slogan would never be accepted by the Israeli population, with the implication that their own separate state would be liquidated and they would be forcibly incorporated into another, 'Palestinian state'.

At the time of writing, because of the brutal, repressive measures of the Sharon regime, and their effects on the Palestinian population, with malnutrition and hunger in the Palestinian areas, the majority of the Palestinians, in despair, seem now to have abandoned hope of a "two-state" solution. One section of the Palestinian bourgeoisie has coupled the idea of the abandonment of the goal of a separate Palestinian state, with the Palestinians fighting for equal rights within the Israeli state. They hope that on the basis of demographic factors – the higher birth rate of the Palestinian population – the Israeli Jews will become a minority within their own state in ten to twenty years' time! Of course, the Israeli bourgeoisie would never accept such a solution. They would opt, if necessary, for the forcible evacuation of even the present Israeli Arabs and the repartition of the area. In other words, a scenario for endless bloody conflict stretching into the far distance would be the consequence of any of the "one-state" solutions on offer. The same applies to the caricature of a genuine "two-state" policy, the proposal of Sharon for what amounts to a "Bantustan" for the Palestinians. Even though, temporarily, the idea of a socialist solution can seem to recede, in the long run it will gather the support of the majority of the Israeli and Palestinian population.

The political, theoretical and organisational backsliding of the ex-CWI members in Scotland has, in turn, become the benchmark for a similar process affecting other organisations formerly claiming to be Marxist. Some of them still formally claim to be under the banner of the "revolutionary left" and even of "Trotskyism". For the Democratic Socialist Party (DSP) in Australia, the International Socialist Tendency and the United Secretariat of the Fourth International (USFI), the approach of the SSP leaders has either served as an "inspiration" for a rightward shift or even as a "model" – the prototype for the kind of party that can be established elsewhere.

From the time of Karl Marx, scientific socialism, with Trotskyism as its expression today, has always seen itself, in the words of the Communist Manifesto, as "The movement of the future in the movement of the present". While always relating to the real level of consciousness and of understanding of the working class, the task of genuine Marxists on issues of programme, tactics and organisation is to direct the gaze of the more developed sections of the working class towards the goal of socialism. Necessarily, this involves the clear demarcation between a consistently Marxist approach and the ideas and methods of left reformism and even centrism, which can develop in periods of sharp social tension. Those who wish to tread in the footsteps of the SSP leaders are in effect sacrificing the future of the working class for short-term gains today.

United Secretariat of the Fourth International (USFI)

On the international plane, the United Secretariat of the Fourth International (USFI) looks towards the SSP, which more and more corresponds to their own view of politics. They are perhaps the most widely known international organisation identified as Trotskyist. Yet, the USFI, by its own admission, claims that at its World Congress in 2003 there were participants from 40 countries (not all of these were members of the USFI). This is a similar figure to the number of different countries in which the CWI has sections, groups or members at present. While the

USFI has a sizeable presence in France, through the LCR, this is not the case in most Western European countries. The strength of the different 'revolutionary left' Internationals is not just a question of present strength but of potential. This, in turn, depends upon a correct analysis of the stage through which society and the working class is passing and all the political conclusions that flow from this. Whether an organisation numbers dozens, hundreds, thousands or even millions is important in relation to the effect it can have, but what is ultimately decisive, when sharp turns in the situation take place, is the political premise of these organisations. It would be criminal to form or maintain a separate political organisation of the left unless there are fundamental differences that cannot be accommodated within one organisation or through the unification of different organisations. At the same time, a revolutionary party is not the same as any transitional broad formation, in which different political positions, organisations and trends, some of them differing wildly from others, can collaborate and work together.

The need for unity flows from the basic trend within the working class to combine its forces against the common enemy, the capitalist class. Woe betides any political party or current that in critical periods stands in the way of this urge for unity! Marxists must always seek common cause, particularly with genuine organisations that have roots in the working class, in specific actions, in united front-type initiatives, etc. But this must not be at the cost of dipping or hiding the Marxist banner, or watering down or not advancing the programme of Marxism. The future of the different 'Internationals' will be determined by their political approach now and in the future and by whether their ideas meet the needs of the current situation.

Neither the IST nor the USFI have ever over a period consistently put forward a Trotskyist or Marxist analysis. The USFI, claiming lineage from Trotsky, is recognised in 'intellectual' circles as the representative of 'orthodox Trotskyism'. Unfortunately, this is not the reality, as an examination of the USFI's current analysis and programme will demonstrate. To take on the designation of 'Trotskyist' is to defend the heritage of Trotsky, his method of analysis and, in general, his activity in the workers' movement. This does not mean a *carte blanche* acceptance of everything that Trotsky did as being right. In a recent series of articles in the USFI's 'International Viewpoint' journal, dedicated to Trotsky, a series of criticisms and attacks on his ideas and methods appeared. Rather than taking up some of the mistakes that Trotsky made – and in his lifetime he admitted to them openly, unlike the USFI and its leaders today – USFI writers attack "mistakes" he never made; they lambast his strong rather than his weak points! In so doing, they echo, unconsciously perhaps, the criticisms of the Stalinists about Trotsky's alleged "weaknesses".

Trotsky and the revolutionary party

Take for instance the question of the need for a party. Francois Vercammen, Secretary of the USFI, wrote an article entitled: "The question of the party: Trotsky's weak point". Vercammen comments: "His weak point is the problem of the party...Trotsky did not have the capacity (1903-1917) or the opportunity (after 1917) to participate directly in the construction of a revolutionary party, in its main aspects (beyond general analyses and perspectives), namely the elaboration and implementation of a political line and concrete tactics, a collective work inside a central leadership, the construction of a political-organisational apparatus, work in common with other cadres and militants; and more generally the implementation of an internal dialectic which prioritises the experience of party militants in the elaboration of a line. Between 1903 and 1917, having broken with Lenin, he did not try to organise a current or a party (confining himself to an activity as a journalist and orator)." [5]

This incredible misinterpretation of Trotsky's position within the Russian Social Democratic Labour Party (RSDLP) reflects the criticisms aimed at Trotsky by bourgeois hacks dabbling in a "sociological" explanation of the revolution. This, in turn, is a reflection of the slanders made by the Stalinists. Trotsky's weakness is not that claimed by Vercammen – a misunderstanding of the need or the character of a party. He participated fully in the RSDLP, which required an understanding of the need for a party and the character of the party at that stage. Vercammen's dismissal of "general analyses and perspectives" ignores Trotsky's major contribution to the success of the socialist revolution – in his monumental work, the book 'Results and Prospects', which explained and developed the 'Theory of Permanent Revolution'. In this, Trotsky correctly anticipated the main forces involved in the first and second Russian Revolutions and, in particular, the decisive role of the working class as the primary force in the alliance with the peasantry, which allowed it to take power in October 1917.

Trotsky's mistake – openly admitted by him, in his 'Diary in Exile', for instance – was not on the issue of the party, the need for such a party, the character of such a party, etc. It was on his "conciliationism", his hope for a reconciliation between Bolshevism and Menshevism between 1907 and 1912. He hoped that, as in the 1905 Revolution, Bolsheviks and Mensheviks would be forced together under the pressure of the masses. Incidentally, he was not alone in this. The ranks of the Bolshevik party put so much pressure on Lenin that on a number of occasions between 1906 and 1912, he was compelled to undertake "unity" negotiations with the Mensheviks. Moreover, Bolsheviks and Mensheviks were united in common organisations in many parts of Russia (outside of Petrograd), up to September 1917. Unlike these particular 'Bolsheviks', Trotsky never entertained political illusions in the

Mensheviks, but sharply and widely diverged from their political programme and perspectives. Therefore, on the political characterisation of the Mensheviks, Trotsky was at one with Lenin. We repeat, where Trotsky made a mistake was not on the question of the party. It was on the illusion that under mass pressure both wings of the RSDLP would be compelled to come together and be forced to accept the main lines of his approach towards the revolution, outlined in the permanent revolution, and the strategy and tactics that would flow from this. Lenin, on the other hand, understood earlier and more clearly that the Mensheviks had already gone over to petty bourgeois and bourgeois conceptions of the coming revolution.

Despite this perception of Lenin's, Trotsky was more correct in his analysis of the coming revolution and particularly the role of the working class as the main agency leading the proletariat to take power, drawing behind it the mass of the peasantry. It is an historical fact that Lenin, in effect, abandoned the 'algebraic formula' of the "democratic dictatorship of the proletariat and the peasantry" after the February Revolution and then, in practice, fully adopted Trotsky's position.

There was no fundamental difference between Trotsky and Lenin in their approach, tactics, strategy, etc, for the revolution. The same could not be said of Stalin, Kamenev or Zinoviev. Vercammen can write, quite absurdly, that: "It was Lenin's determination to attach himself to the 'real movement' in Russia, combined with a succession of complex socio-political conjunctures, which fashioned and rooted the Bolshevik party in [urban] Russian society. It was the policy of Lenin which was determinant and not his 'conception' of the party, such as is commonly understood (Democratic Centralism, The General Programme)... It was the political weakness of Trotsky which was at the base of his defeat at the level of the organisation. One can follow it up in the following manner: before 1917, his extraordinary capacity to grasp the significant general tendencies of the era and to draw strategic perspectives did not allow him to develop a revolutionary policy (and he was unable or unwilling to create a militant collective). His weakness on the party is located in this framework."

And yet, as we have stated, Trotsky rather than Lenin had the clearest perspective of the forces and the outcome of the Russian revolution. Vercammen lauds Lenin's policy quite correctly in relation to 1917 – and yet speaks of "Trotsky's political weaknesses". And all of this, which we have answered many times before against Stalinists, is part of an alleged defence of Trotsky! The roots of his latter-day criticism of Trotsky's alleged mistakes flow from the incapacity of the USFI itself to build sizeable organisations in the past. Vercammen points to the failure of his organisation in 1965-68, and compares it to the period of 1895-1914, when Lenin was able to establish an outline of the revolutionary party which matured and took power in October 1917. Unfortunately, Vercammen misunderstands the whole character of the 1965-68 period and its different conjunctures. Stalinism and social democracy, he claims, began to "break up" in the period prior to the May events of 1968. This is just not true. Reformist organisations and the consciousness that goes with them still, in general, held a grip on the minds of the masses in this period. For us,as Marxists, social democratic and mass Stalinist parties were an objective factor, which could only be overcome by events. This happened to some extent in the revolutionary events in France of May-June 1968. However, the absence of a mass revolutionary party and leadership at this time allowed the Stalinist French Communist Party and the reformist 'Socialists' to re-establish their control and derail this potential revolution.

In Britain, during the 1970s and 1980s, Militant, the forerunner of the Socialist Party, made breakthroughs in Liverpool and in the anti-Poll Tax struggle. Unfortunately, as we have explained elsewhere, this promising beginning to the building of a mass revolutionary party was cut across by the boom of the 1980s and, of course, by the collapse of Stalinism. Vercammen's rewriting of Trotsky's role and Trotsky's alleged 'weakness' on organisation and the party, etc, combined with his sublimated political criticisms, betrays an impatient approach to the problem of assembling the outline of a party and building such a force. This task involves understanding the different stages through which the working class and its level of understanding will pass. It means being prepared to stand against the stream in certain periods, at the risk of being accused of being sectarian. But it also means assembling a working-class cadre, rooting the party in the working class neighbourhoods and organisations – trade unions, co-operative societies, etc. – and seizing the opportunities to create a mass or semi-mass base, as and when they arise.

Incredibly, Vercammen accuses Trotsky of being "indecisive and confused (even after 1905) on the question of electoral support to the liberal bourgeoisie". This is done without any attempt to explain what Vercammen means by this. However, when it comes to the question of the peasantry, he directly attacks Trotsky and thereby one of the main elements of Trotsky's theory of the permanent revolution. Vercammen states: "In 1906, and the years that followed, he satisfied himself with two theoretical generalisations which translated above all the prejudices of European Marxism at the time (post-Marx): historically, the countryside follows the town and the peasantry the proletariat (industrial, urbanised); at the same time, the peasantry is incapable of following an autonomous political line and creating an independent organisation". He goes on further to echo the criticisms of the Stalinists, and the latter-day theoretical 'Stalinists' of the DSP in Australia, in arguing: "Trotsky did not seek, unlike Lenin, the construction of a real workers' and peasants' alliance, with all its demands. By its abstract character, the theory proved a veritable trap for Trotsky"[6] This is merely an echo of the Stalinists' argument on the "underestimation" by Trotsky of the revolutionary potential of the proletariat.

The Permanent Revolution

Asimilar point is made by Michael Lowy in International Viewpoint, allegedly defending the theory of the permanent revolution. The author writes: "The theory of the permanent revolution has been verified twice in the course of the history of the 20th century. On the one hand, by the disasters resulting from stageism, from the blind application by the Communist parties in the dependent countries, of the Stalinist doctrine of the revolution by stages and the bloc with the national bourgeoisie, from Spain in 1936 to Indonesia in 1965 or Chile in 1973."[7]

Michael Lowy then goes on to say that the theory has been verified on the other hand, "Because this theory, such as it was formulated from 1906, has largely allowed us to predict, explain and shed light on the revolutions of the 20th century, which have all been 'permanent' revolutions in the peripheral countries. What happened in Russia, China, Yugoslavia, Vietnam or Cuba has corresponded, in its broad outlines, to Trotsky's central idea: the possibility of combined and uninterrupted revolution – democratic and socialist – in a country of peripheral capitalism, dependent or colonial. The fact that, overall, the leaders of the revolutionary movements after October 1917 have not recognised the 'permanent' character of these latter (with some exceptions, like Ernesto Che Guevara), or have done it *a posteriori* and employing a different terminology, takes nothing away from this historically effective relation…

"Today as yesterday, the revolutionary transformations which are on the agenda in the societies at the periphery of the system are not identical with those of the countries of the centre. A social revolution in India could not be, from the point of view of its programme, strategy and motor forces, a pure 'workers' revolution' as in England. The decisive political role – certainly not envisaged by Trotsky! – played in many countries today by the indigenous and peasant movements (the FZLN in Mexico, the Brazilian MST, the CONAIE in Ecuador) shows the importance and social explosiveness of the agrarian question, and its close link with national liberation."[8]

Both points are entirely wrong. Firstly, Trotsky understood the importance of mobilising the peasantry, particularly in Russia where the proletariat was a small minority. But he was absolutely right in understanding that the peasantry was heterogeneous and incapable of independently coming to power and maintaining that power. In a sense, Lowy is correct that the theory of permanent revolution has been borne out by the victory of the revolution in China, Yugoslavia, Vietnam, and Cuba. But these victories do so, not in the classical sense implied by Lowy, but as a caricature. Apart from Russia in 1917, the working class did not directly take power, or establish independent workers' organisations – soviets, etc. Mobilising the peasants in the Chinese Revolution, a Bonapartist clique, led by Mao Zedong, was able to take power, balancing between the classes and constructing a state, which from the outset was a Stalinist regime in the image of Stalin's Russia.

This is not recognised in the USFI's analysis of the processes which led to the creation of these states. Because of this, they make fundamental mistakes on the issue of the 'peasantry'. As we show in 'The History of the CWI', this resulted in the USFI making a number of gross errors in the past on the issue of guerrillaist tactics, the role of the peasantry in the revolution, etc. It has led the USFI to support guerrillaist adventures in Uruguay and Argentina, where some of the flower of the youth were wasted in futile military conflict with the state, over the heads of the working class. The USFI also gave uncritical support to the IRA in Ireland, and pursued many other adventures.

Unfortunately, the USFI have not learnt from their mistakes, as is now illustrated by Lowy's comments on Trotsky's alleged position on the peasantry. He states: "The principle limitation of Trotsky's analysis is of a 'sociological' rather than strategic nature: to consider the peasantry uniquely as a 'support' of the revolutionary proletariat as a class of 'small proprietors' whose horizon did not go beyond democratic demands. He had trouble in accepting, for example, a Chinese Red Army composed in its great majority of peasants. His error – like most Russian and European Marxists – was to adopt, without critical examination, Marx's analysis in 'The Eighteenth Brumaire' of the French peasantry as an atomised and petty bourgeois class and to apply it to colonial and semi-colonial nations with very different characteristics. However, in one of his last writings, 'Preconceptions of the Russian Revolution' (1939), Trotsky argued that the Marxist appreciation of the peasantry as a non-socialist class had never had an 'absolute and immutable' character."[9]

These criticisms of Trotsky are wrong from beginning to end. The precise balance within the peasantry between smallholders or proprietors, poor peasants and landless labourers, who tend to sink into the ranks of the proletariat, differs from continent to continent, and even from country to country. However, the general Marxist proposition, from Marx himself, about the heterogeneous character of the peasantry retains its full validity in relation to the neo-colonial world today. Marx's brilliant idea, that only the working class, organised in large industry, disciplined by the factory or the workplace, can develop the necessary social cohesion and, ultimately, the necessary consciousness, to carry through a socialist overturn, has been borne out in all revolutions. This was the case principally in the Russian Revolution, but also applies even where revolutions have not taken a 'classical' form, as in China.

China, Yugoslavia and Cuba

In fact, Trotsky's writings on China, particularly his characterisation of Mao Zedong's 'Red Army' in the 1930s, were brilliantly accurate. He pointed out that this was a rural echo of the defeated workers' revolution of 1925-27. The ex-communists who were leading this movement, he said, could develop over a period a certain suspicion and hostility towards the working class, even if they were victorious and entered the cities. This was because they were conditioned to a rural existence amongst the peasant masses, on which they were based. Is this not what happened when the Red Army defeated the Kuo Min Tang and took over the major cities of China? Before they occupied the cities, they called for the masses not to rise, warning that strikes would be punished. There were no soviets, independent organisations of the working class or of the peasantry, for that matter. Trotsky held out the prospect that, like all peasant movements throughout history, the Chinese Red Army could be victorious, could defeat the Kuo Min Tang but that it would remain within the framework of capitalism. This could result in the setting up of another dynasty, which would degenerate into a bourgeois feudal regime and so the process of opposition and peasant revolution would begin once more.

That events in China did not happen in this fashion was largely accounted for by the balance of world forces, manifested in China. Chronically weak, the bourgeoisie and the landlords had fled from China with the defeated armies of Chiang Kai Shek. In the vacuum that was left, Mao represented a Bonapartist clique at the head of a victorious army. The clique manoeuvred between the classes but was compelled by the pressure from below to carry through the expropriation of landlordism and capitalism, largely from above. Nowhere in Trotsky will you read what Lowy implies, that the peasantry, particularly the lowest layers, the poor peasants etc., were impervious to the ideas of socialism. Even during the Russian Revolution, as John Reed points out in his book, 'Ten Days That Shook the World', peasant soldiers saw the October Revolution as the beginning of a *world, socialist* overturn. Moreover, in parts of the neo-colonial world today, such is the desperation of the peasantry, with their small and unviable plots of land, the idea of co-operatives and the general ideas of 'socialism' can prove attractive, particularly when advocated by parties with powerful roots in the industrial urban working class. However, the peasantry – the 'countryside' – would still need to find a leading force in the towns if a socialist overturn is to be accomplished and consolidated, and then appeals would also have to be made to the working class internationally.

Marx, and Trotsky after him, described the limitations of the peasantry and its scattered, stratified character; as a class it would not be able to play an independent role. It could, nevertheless, play a vital and necessary auxiliary role in supporting an industrial, revolutionary movement of the urban working class to take power. Undoubtedly, where the working class is a minority in society, a classical working class uprising could be "supplemented" by a "second edition of the peasant war" – a movement of the peasants, even including elements of guerrillaism. The CWI, following Trotsky's method of analysis, however, made clear differentiations.

Guerrillaist methods used in the countryside amongst the rural population, as an auxiliary to the movement of the working class in the industrial areas, are quite different from using them as a method of struggle equally applicable amongst workers. This should be basic ABC for Marxists and particularly those claiming to be Trotskyists. Unfortunately, however, the USFI on this, and on other issues, is guilty of theoretical backsliding. In practice, this can lead to further disasters in the future, if the USFI were to become influential in mass movements.

The same applies to the USFI's characterisation of what they call "bureaucratised" regimes. They claim that they have always been critical of regimes such as Yugoslavia under Tito, Cuba, China, etc. However, these 'criticisms' were in the context of accepting that these were basically relatively healthy workers' states. If elements of 'bureaucratism' existed, they were the 'same kind' of bureaucratic distortions as existed when Russia was a healthy workers' state in the period 1917-23, Ernest Mandel, the former theoretical leader of the USFI, argued insistently against the CWI. We fundamentally disagreed with this analysis.[10] We opposed, for instance, the USFI's implication that Tito was an "unconscious Trotskyist". This involved the sending of "volunteers" to Yugoslavia when Tito clashed with Stalin in 1949. However, Tito was a "national Stalinist", who came into collision with Stalin not over the character of his regime (since Tito's was modelled on Moscow) but as an expression of the national Stalinist opposition of the Yugoslav bureaucracy to 'Big Brother' in Moscow.

The same approach was adopted by the USFI at the time of the Sino-Soviet dispute in the late 1950s and early 1960s. At that stage, Mandel believed that an "anti-bureaucratic revolution" – that is, a political revolution – was no longer necessary in China because Mao's regime was a relatively healthy workers' state with some mild bureaucratic deformations. Such a position is untenable today, given the revelations – the crimes, in fact – committed by Mao and his heirs in suppressing the demands of the Chinese masses for basic democratic rights.

In relation to Cuba, the same mistaken approach was employed by the USFI leaders. This revolution was a huge blow to imperialism. We, as well as the USFI, enthusiastically supported the revolution. We recognised the massive effect it had throughout the world and particularly in Latin America and the neo-colonial world. However, the origins of the Cuban Revolution were somewhat different from the Chinese Revolution, with the Castro regime occupying and still enjoying a popular base. Nevertheless, the masses still do not possess independent means of exercising control and power; there was and is no right of recall over officials, no election of officials, no clear limited wage differentials between those at the top and workers.[11] We have consistently defended Cuba from the attacks of imperialism but, at the same time, call for the institution of real workers' democracy as the only guarantee of being able to mobilise support – in Cuba, Latin America and throughout the world – from the threats made by imperialism and its attempt to return Cuba back to capitalism. It is quite wrong now, as in a resolution adopted at the 15th World Congress of the USFI in the summer of 2003, for the USFI to claim: "We have always combated the bureaucratic regimes that claimed to be socialist while maintaining the oppressive regimes against peoples and workers, in the name of rights to self-organisation, workers' self-management and democracy." As welcome as it is for the USFI leaders to conclude this now, this has clearly not been the case in the above-cited cases. It is easy after the fact, when the character of regimes has been clearly shown to be bureaucratic, to make this or that criticism. But the USFI, right from the inception of the Cuban revolution, never came out with a clear Trotskyist analysis. This includes supporting the anti-imperialist, anticapitalist measures taken by Castro and the establishment of a planned economy with all the enormous benefits this has meant to the Cuban people compared to the discredited Batista regime. The USFI did this, but, at the same time, they refused to call for soviets and all the other demands essential for a healthy workers' state and the beginning of a move towards socialism.

Lost opportunities in France

In Europe, the USFI's most prominent national section is the Ligue Communiste Révolutionnaire (LCR – Revolutionary Communist League), in France. On a number of occasions since 1995, including in recent elections, the opportunity has existed to take decisive steps towards the formation of a new mass workers' party. The LCR together with Lutte Ouvrière (LO) seemed to be attracting significant support from young people and workers protesting at the shift to the right of the 'pluralist left', the Socialist Party (PS), in the main, but also the French Communist Party (PCF). For instance, in January 2004, two months before the French regional elections, polls indicated that 9% of the French population would vote for the LO/LCR candidates and another 22% were seriously considering it. However, the LO/LCR alliance suffered a serious setback. It polled only 3.3% of the vote in the European elections and lost all its 5 MEPs. A short-term squeezing of the vote of the smaller left parties can sometimes occur when voters flock to an opposition that is seen as the 'lesser evil', so as to defeat the parties of the right. However, LO/LCR ran a lacklustre campaign, which was deficient in putting forward fighting demands and a clear explanation of a socialist alternative. They attacked the parties of the 'traditional left', such as the ex-social democratic PS, and described them as 'social-liberals' – whatever that means! But they did not raise the idea of a new workers' party as a socialist alternative to the bourgeois parties. It was discarded as something for after the elections; in the meantime another opportunity has been lost.

What is needed is an active campaign and plan of action for the formation of a new workers' party. Two years previously, the combined vote of LO and LCR reached

10.4% in the first round of the presidential elections, such was the opposition to the outgoing PS/PCF government. The movement against Jean Marie Le Pen, who reached the second round of the presidential elections by beating the then prime minister Jospin into third place, was an enormous opportunity to initiate a lively broad campaign for a new workers' party.

Instead, the LCR, by adopting the slogan, "Fight the National Front in the streets and in the polling stations', did not present an independent working class position and allowed the working class to be mobilised behind Chirac, the incumbent president. Chirac, who received less than 20% of the vote in the first round of the presidential elections, and who was widely seen as totally corrupt, came out of the second round with 82.15% of the vote. This formed the basis for a second election victory for the right and the subsequent formation of a government with the confidence to attack fundamental workers' rights, like welfare and pension 'reforms'.

In May and June 2003, there was another opportunity to form a new workers' party. The protests against the government's pension reform led to a situation of a near general strike, with millions demonstrating against the right-wing Raffarin government. The need for a mass party defending the rights of workers and the poor was in the forefront of everyone's mind, as nobody believed the parties of the 'Gauche plurielle' (PS, PCF and Greens) had any alternative to offer.

In an opinion poll taken the week after the massive demonstration on Sunday 25 May 2003, 47% said they thought the PS would be neither better nor worse in dealing with pension reform (47% said the same on education reform and 50% on health reform). At demonstrations a layer of the workers' blamed the radical left for calling for a Chirac vote in the presidential elections a year earlier – saying that this had lead to a stronger right-wing government. In the aftermath of the struggle against pension reform, when trade union leaders only just saved the government by avoiding a general strike, attention switched again to the political stage.[12]

The revolutionary party today

As well as the USFI's mistakes in France and elsewhere, the organisation has thrown out fundamental principles of revolutionary organisation; rejecting Lenin and Trotsky's conception of the revolutionary party and the revolutionary International; instead they favour broader formations like Rifondazione Comunista (RC) in Italy and the Scottish Socialist Party (SSP). Of course, it is not sufficient in the present period, marked by capitalist globalisation and post-Stalinism, to merely repeat by rote formulas from the past. This is as true in the sphere of organisation as in political ideas. In explaining the need for organisation, it has been particularly important to take account of the new generation's suspicion of any 'top-down' organisation. Amongst this layer there is a pronounced reaction against the bureaucratic character of both Stalinism and the ex-social democracy, which anyway, on the organisational level, imitates Stalinism. This has sometimes taken the form of a sweeping rejection of 'organisation' in general and even of 'politics', at least of bourgeois politics, and the concept of a 'party'. Marxists are therefore compelled to take account of this. Unfortunately, in some cases this has gone too far, involving an attempt to adapt in an opportunist fashion to passing and transient moods. For the USFI, this borders on a rejection of the past, both of their own organisation and of the historical contribution of Trotsky and 'Trotskyism' to the struggles of the working class.

As an example, take the writings of Daniel Bensaïd, one of the theoreticians of the LCR in France, the best known section of the USFI. He comments on what he claims was, "One of the most debatable characteristics of Leninism, democratic centralism".[13]

In the 1990s, Marxism came under ferocious attack as it does even now and the CWI has been prepared to debate Lenin's conception of the party, the character of the party that he built in Russia and its application to the workers' struggle today. The centralist aspect was undoubtedly emphasised by Lenin and the Bolsheviks because of the underground struggle against the Tsarist dictatorship. At the same time, the Bolshevik Party was extremely democratic – the most democratic mass workers' party in history. Without this democratic element – fully displayed particularly in the period between February and October 1917 – the working class, or its most advanced layers, would not have found a home within that party. Nor would the masses have transferred their hopes and support to the Bolsheviks, which led to the October Revolution. At one stage in the 1990s, the CWI took account of the prejudices against the idea of democratic centralism, distorted by the heritage of Stalinism – bureaucratic centralism – and proposed using instead the phrase "democratic unity". However, it soon became clear that this phrase confused rather than enlightened; we were compelled to revert to Lenin's phrase, which does, when it is properly explained, reflect what the working class demands from their organisations in struggle.

Workers' organisations need and demand the maximum amount of democracy, particularly in the present period, when the capitalist class promotes worldwide illusions in bourgeois democracy. At the same time, the capitalists have concentrated and centralised their power, economically and also in their state machine. Spontaneous, semi-spontaneous and anarchist conceptions of organisation against this concentrated force of the capitalists, is not only inadequate but can be fatal in the serious struggles of the working class, which impend in the next decade. A genuine democratic, centralised revolutionary party is not akin to the Stalinist model. That was top-down, bureaucratic centralist, dominated from the top by self-appointed leaders, a party caste. In the modern era this model is imitated by the ex-social democratic leaders, as in Blair's New Labour Party. This party is an undemocratic, as well as bureaucratic, nightmare compared to twenty years ago, when the Labour Party was at least partially a vehicle for the struggles of working class people in Britain.

The new generation of young people and workers, it is true, do not want a rigidly controlled party, in which the leadership is omnipresent and supposedly omniscient. For instance, a new mass workers' party in Britain, of necessity, would have to have some of the features of the Labour Party in its formative period and in its 'best days'. Namely, it should be broad and federal in character – because of the different strands that would be represented initially – and welcoming to all those who would be prepared to struggle on the basis of a basic socialist programme.

On the other hand, a revolutionary party is not a transitional formation, as is the case with a new mass workers' party. It represents the coming together of the most conscious revolutionary forces, who have understood the need to create the embryo of a combat party, which can take on mass proportions at a later stage.

Such revolutionary parties today would not be on the strict pattern of Lenin's concept for Russia in the early part of the twentieth century. The revolutionary party would borrow heavily from the tremendous example of the Bolshevik party but would add to those past experiences the democratic traditions and methods of the working class in each country. How it would conduct itself internally – through debates and discussions, the latitude that would be given to organised minorities within the party, how this would be expressed, not just internally but publicly – are all issues to be debated and discussed in the course of the creation of such parties. But one thing is absolutely certain: while maximum democracy and discussion are necessary, so also is the need to act in unison once decisions are taken. This elementary concept is understood, for example, by every serious worker involved in a strike, where majority decisions impose discipline upon the minority, and they have to accept the decisions and act on them. It is fundamentally no different when it comes to the actions of a revolutionary party.

This approach towards building the party has been unfortunately abandoned by the USFI and replaced by a concept which involves virtually 'anything goes' – an extremely loose organisational form. The same applies to the question of a new mass International. What would be the character of such an International and how would it be built? The USFI's answer is to throw overboard the real lessons of Lenin and Trotsky's contribution on this issue. Unfortunately, they have opportunistically bent to the pressures of the 1990s, which have been carried over into the first part of this century. This becomes clear when examining the 'balance sheet' the USFI leaders have drawn about their past experiences, the character of a party and the International that is required in the modern era. At the recent USFI World Congress, the leaders come out for, "The constitution of a new internationalist, pluralist, revolutionary, militant force with a mass impact". They explain: "This assertion implies a significant revision of what the Fourth International could carry out. It is not 'the World Party of Socialist Revolution' (the objective adopted at the time of its founding) or even the central nucleus of such a future party. The 65 years that separate us from this proclamation have not been marked by a process of gathering of the revolutionary forces but by ruptures, separated groups, and splits. We are one Trotskyist current among others, one revolutionary current among others. The chapter is closed when the Fourth International could have the perspective of being carried to the head of the revolutionary process, with the help of a huge militant effort, a correct analysis and a successful battle inside the Trotskyist movement".[14]

In other documents the USFI state that the model which they are aiming for is something similar to the First International, that is a broad, pluralist but not specifically Marxist or Trotskyist International. It is true that the CWI, in discussions with the USFI and others in the early 1990s, suggested that, in the light of the new situation which was posed before the Trotskyist movement and the workers' movement, in general, an international organisation or forum similar to the First International could play an important role. This could help in the process of theoretical clarification, working out the basis for common work, etc. But we never perceived this as the finished article, the ultimate goal of revolutionary Marxists. It was seen as a transitional organisation – as Marx and Engels had originally perceived the First International – towards a firmer ideological organisation later, based on the ideas of scientific socialism. To return to the concept of the First International as the finished historical model for the working class is a mistake. If such an organisation came into being, we would participate. We would not, however, dissolve our forces but maintain our distinct ideas and programme, as well as organisation, within such a formation. In other words, as with the conception of new, broad, mass workers' parties on a national scale, such an International would not constitute, as Tony Benn, a leading left figure in Britain, and others have envisaged, a 'Fifth International'. It would be more of the coming together of different organisations, a federal form of organisation which could allow collaboration, discussion and some common actions. Yet it would not be an end in itself, certainly as far as Marxists and Trotskyists are concerned.

It is quite clear that the USFI has given up on the idea of an International – leave aside its name for the moment – which aims to become the 'World Party of Socialist Revolution'. The USFI even maintains that it does not even aim to be the "central nucleus of such a party" or International. The justification for this is the alleged "failures" of Trotsky's original concept of a mass revolutionary Fourth International. As we pointed out in the History of the CWI, the failure of such an International to develop was because of the objective realities of the outcome of the Second World War, together with the mistakes of the leaders of the USFI (following the death of

Trotsky) at key periods of its history. The CWI has never believed that the realisation of Trotsky's idea of a mass International would be achieved just by "militant effort, a correct analysis and a successful battle inside the Trotskyist movement".[15]

A new revolutionary Fourth International will be the product of a clarity of ideas, which takes as its starting point the methods of Trotsky and of the International Left Opposition, continually updated and sharpened, plus the addition of new fresh mass forces. The precondition for this is the emergence of a new generation of young people and workers who, through experience, will see the need, specifically, for such a revolutionary party.

IST/SWP

The International Socialist Tendency (IST), whose most prominent group is the Socialist Workers' Party (SWP) in Britain, is another example of so-called Trotskyists making political and tactical blunders which can seriously damage the movement of workers and young people to end capitalism. The IST/SWP operated throughout most of the 1990s from a polar opposite position to that of the USFI; they were ultra-left and sectarian. However, they have recently moved towards the right, and are increasingly occupying the same political ground as the USFI.

The IST/SWP political views on the collapse of the Berlin Wall were completely at variance with what actually flowed from this turning point in history. According to them, nothing fundamental had happened to decisively alter the reality confronting Marxists. They were blissfully unaware that the consciousness of the working class had been affected by these events. Yet, as we have seen, this was not the view of the bourgeoisie at the time or now, as the comments of Greenspan quoted earlier indicate. Moreover, anyone with roots in the working class and its organisations could not fail to register the changes that had taken place – the difficulties now encountered by socialists faced with a barrage of attacks against the ideas of 'socialism', let alone Marxism and Trotskyism.

In effect, the IST sought to defy the laws of political gravity with their employment of 'voluntarist' methods. These brought them some success in the short term by appealing primarily to students and the radicalised petty bourgeois, whose milieu was isolated from the real moods and outlook of working class people. But their misreading of the situation flowed from the false theoretical basis of this organisation: the 'theory' of 'state capitalism', as enunciated by their major theoretician, the late Tony Cliff – a 'theory' which he initially applied to Stalinist Russia, Eastern Europe, China, etc. These ideas were at complete variance with the ideas of Trotsky, as outlined in his monumental work 'In Defence of Marxism'. The CWI also consistently opposed this theory. It was answered very thoroughly in Ted Grant's 'Against the Theory of State Capitalism'[16] and, more recently, in Peter

Hadden's 'The Struggle for Socialism Today: A Reply to the Politics of the Socialist Workers Party' [17] and Sascha Stanicic's 'Welcher Weg zum Sozialismus?' [18], as well as in other publications of the CWI.

The IST/SWP, although it claims on occasions to be 'Trotskyist', has diverged quite decisively from the theoretical heritage of Trotsky, particularly in relation to the key issue of the class character of the states of Eastern Europe and the Soviet Union when under the control of Stalinist bureaucracies. In that sense, they cannot be considered as a genuine continuation of the Trotskyist tradition.

A theoretical error, particularly on such a crucial issue as the class character of the Soviet Union, will sooner or later be reflected in false policies, methods and organisation. This is the case even when the Stalinist state, the Soviet Union, which was the origin of this error, has collapsed. What is revealed is a false approach. This is quite clearly the case with the IST/SWP. The countries of Eastern Europe and the former Soviet Union were, according to them, 'state capitalist' and therefore their collapse did not register with the IST as an historic setback for the working class. It was merely a 'sideways move', the replacement of one capitalist regime by another.

This led to false conclusions being drawn by the IST's German section. In relation to the events of 1989 and the fall of the Berlin Wall, it stated: "Instead of defending the independence of the GDR [East Germany] at any price socialists would have had the task to push forward the real workers' struggles. A general strike against the Stasi and for a referendum on unification would have been possible at the beginning of December (1989). A revolutionary transitional government arising out of a general strike would have had the task to fully dissolve the Stasi and the old power apparatus and negotiate the conditions for a reunification with the Kohl government". [19]

In other words, the IST's German section supported capitalist re-unification, with all the terrible problems which have resulted from this for the German, and particularly the East German, workers. The liquidation of the planned economy – albeit mangled and distorted by Stalinism in decline – was of no consequence to this 'Tendency'. It therefore followed for them that these events in no way altered the level of understanding and the consciousness of the working class.

This surreal interpretation of the situation following the fall of the Berlin Wall differs fundamentally with the conclusions mentioned above. These include the views of the advanced layers of the working class, within the unions, in the social-democratic parties, and particularly in the 'Communist' parties at the time. In the long run, it is true, the discrediting of Stalinism, which has historically besmirched the labour movement with its dirty methods, purges, mass expulsions, frame-ups etc., will prove to be progressive. But the state-owned planned economies of Eastern Europe and the Soviet Union, despite the monstrous totalitarian character of Stalinism, were relatively progressive compared with capitalism. To paraphrase

Trotsky, it was in the language of steel, concrete and cement, with a spectacular growth rate in the initial period, at least, that these economies showed the advantages of state ownership and planning over outmoded, chaotic, anarchic capitalism. Their liquidation was keenly felt by the advanced socialist and communist layers of the working class. For opposite reasons, this process was celebrated by the strategists of world capitalism. But to the IST, it was of no fundamental consequence!

The Transitional Programme

Now the IST, despite its formal adherence to the goal of a 'revolutionary party', has followed the USFI through a blatant opportunist turn, particularly in Britain. This seems to be in marked contrast to their policies in the 1990s. Reality, however, always imposes itself, even belatedly, on those in political denial. Towards the end of the 1990s, the IST came up against a political brick wall. The SWP was compelled to moderate its previous crude sectarian ultra-leftism – "no participation in elections", "smash the state" etc., which Peter Hadden took up effectively in his pamphlet, 'The Struggle for Socialism Today: A Reply to the Politics of the Socialist Workers Party'.

In the manner of pre-1914 social democracy, the SWP put forward the 'maximum' programme – the call for revolution and socialism, "smash the state" – together with the 'minimum' programme of day-to-day reforms. The 'maximum' and 'minimum' programmes are separated in the agitation and propaganda of the SWP. Trotsky, on the contrary, basing himself on the experiences of the Bolshevik Party, put forward a programme of transitional demands in the 1930s. This flowed from the economic situation pertaining then, in which capitalism could no longer afford lasting reforms. Therefore, the struggle for reforms, seriously conducted, posed the need for the socialist transformation of society.

Trotsky's series of 'transitional demands' were a bridge from the existing level of consciousness of the working class at that stage to the idea of the socialist transformation of society. But the IST, beginning with Tony Cliff, rejected this idea. Cliff made his organisation's view clear: "The basic assumption behind Trotsky's transitional demands was that the economic crisis was so deep that the struggle for even the smallest improvement in workers' conditions would bring conflict with the capitalist system itself. When life disproved the assumption the ground fell from beneath the programme."[20]

No programme is put forward irrespective of the concrete historical conditions. Trotsky's approach was entirely justified in the 1930s. But what Cliff did not understand was the change in the objective situation which flowed from the world upswing of capitalism in the post-1945 period, which did allow serious reforms to be conquered by the working class. Even then, contrary to Cliff's assertion, the working class did actually implement some of the transitional demands outlined by Trotsky. For instance, for an historical period the Italian workers implemented the idea of a sliding scale of wages, through the *scala mobile*. The colossal development of the shop stewards' committees in Britain, in the post WW2 period, and in other countries, was a partial realisation, in a slightly different form, of the demand in Trotsky's programme for "factory committees".

But the conditions sketched out by Trotsky in the 1930s are beginning to mature today. There is an organic world economic crisis of capitalism, which has compelled the ruling class to engage in a ferocious attack on living standards, as described earlier. This means that the struggle for lasting reforms inevitably poses the question of the revolutionary transformation of society. In no way does this mean that important short-term gains by the working class are not possible but they are temporary and cannot have a lasting character, given the inevitable attempts by capitalism to take them back. Witness the stubborn insistence of the French ruling class – despite the fact they have been defeated time and again over ten years of efforts – to cut the living standards of the French workers and to even take back the 35-hour week, a conquest of a previous period.

Therefore, just when the method of Trotsky is beginning to come into its own, although the type of programme and many of its demands will be different today because of the different conditions, the SWP rejects it. In the past, they accused the CWI, particularly 'Militant' (now the Socialist Party) in Britain, of capitulating to 'reformism'. This was never the case; we indissolubly connected the day-to-day demands of the working class with the idea of the socialist goal, specifically mentioning the contribution of Marx, Engels, Lenin and Trotsky. Sometimes the SWP may still shout about "Revolution!" but more often then not now their day-to-day activity consists of limiting their programme to minimum slogans like "Tax the rich!" This goes hand-in-hand with an uncritical approach towards leading 'Left' figures.

Another example of the IST's attitude is the pamphlet 'Anti-Capitalism' by leading SWP member, Chris Harman. This deals in great length with the anti-capitalist movement but does not make a single programmatical proposal and does not mention socialism once. Nowhere does Harman call for the nationalisation of the multinational corporations under democratic workers' control and management. Nowhere does he put forward a democratically planned economy as an alternative to the market system. He deals with the anti-capitalist movement and the workers' movement as if they were two completely separated things which cannot be brought together. The necessity of new workers' parties with a socialist programme is not mentioned.

SWP's electoralism

Previously, the SWP accused the CWI of 'electoralism'. This was never true. For instance, in all the election campaigns mounted in Liverpool in the 1980s, in Coventry, past and present, or in the successful parliamentary campaigns of Joe Higgins, in Ireland, socialism, the need for a democratic, planned, socialist economy, was prominently featured. The SWP have not put a clear case for socialism in the election campaigns they have been involved in.

This is manifested in Britain by their leadership's uncritical support and advocacy of George Galloway's 'Respect Unity' coalition. This has now involved them in arguing against advancing the case for "socialism" in their eagerness for electoral success. A striking example of their reluctance to mention the 'S' word was provided by Alex Callinicos, a professor at York University in northern England, and a central leader of the SWP. He was invited to participate on Sunday 30 June, 2003, in a debate on the BBC Radio 4 programme, 'Broadcasting House', with Ruth Lea, Head of Policy at the British bosses' organisation, the Institute of Directors, and Robert Kelsey, the pro-capitalist author. Towards the end of this radio discussion, Callinicos was asked what his alternative to capitalism was. Not once did he even mention socialism. In fact, he sounded like a liberal. His answer began by simply saying that it was time to "move beyond capitalism". Callinicos went on to say, "We're going to create an alternative model," and he promised that, "We will come up with a more promising way to run the world". Finally, when challenged by the others that he was arguing for something like Stalinist North Korea, all Callinicos could say was there were "plenty of better ways to run the world". The question arises whether Callinicos is becoming a 'post-socialist' or does the SWP think that the word 'socialism' can only be spoken in limited circles, and certainly not on national radio?

In his recent book, 'Anti-Capitalist Manifesto', the demands Callinicos puts forward are completely within the framework of the capitalist system. He demands capital controls but does not raise the need for the nationalisation of the big banks and big industries. The question of economic planning seems to be raised in the book but not as part of the transitional programme. His 'transitional programme' also does not include any demands for the labour movement and no proposals for a strategy for the working class. Callinicos writes that these demands should mean improvements here and now but also should start to invent "a different social logic".

The IST grouping shows a similar attitude to the discussion in 2004 on the need for a new left party in Germany. They openly came out against not only a socialist programme for the new party (known in June 2004 as 'Election Alternative – Work and Social Justice') but also against even a debate within the new formation on that question. They claimed that this would be a barrier for new layers to join. On at least three occasions, IST members have intervened openly against CWI members and others who wanted to raise the "system question" and they supported the reformists.

In the anti-capitalist struggle, for instance in Genoa, the IST/SWP's main slogan was "Another world is possible". But they did not even attempt to link this to the idea of a socialist world. Bob Labi, a member of the International Secretariat of the CWI who participated in this demonstration, comments: "Their Irish contingent [in Genoa] had a placard calling for 'Fair Trade not Free Trade', a utopian demand under capitalism that, in reality, implies asking for a 'nicer' capitalism. When challenged on this slogan, one of their Irish leaders replied: 'Why can't you enjoy this wonderful event? Look how many people are here, don't spoil it.'

"Moreover, the German IST grouping, Linksruck, produced a special nine-page briefing for their members under the title, 'A different world is possible! – Info briefing for the G8 Summit protests in Genoa'. This document, while stressing building an anti-capitalist movement with strong local roots, did not raise the question of how to develop this movement into a socialist one. In fact, the word 'socialist' is not used anywhere in this briefing."

In Britain, the main spokespersons of the IST have specifically argued against using the word 'socialism'. Lindsey German of the SWP in Britain argued against its inclusion in the 'Respect' coalition programme, because, allegedly, the 'Socialist Alliance' had failed in elections because it stood on a socialist platform! Needless to say, this switch in 'politics' did not extend to the SWP's methods and approach towards other groups, which have been as overbearing as ever.

An indication of the IST's complete inability to correctly estimate a situation is how Alex Callinicos, their major theoretician since the death of Tony Cliff, could write, in March 2002, about the "Isolation [of] revolutionary socialists... for the past twenty years."[21] This encompasses the period in Britain during which the miners' strike of 1984-85, the magnificent anti-poll tax movement, organised and led by Militant, and the tumultuous upheavals in the British Labour Party around the figure of Tony Benn and the emergence of a powerful left wing, all took place! This was a period of isolation not for genuine revolutionary socialists but for the sectarian SWP/IST, who were reduced to shouting from the sidelines at real movements of the working class. For instance, when Liverpool City Council humbled Thatcher in 1984 and extracted big concessions from the government, the SWP denounced the City Council in their paper, 'Socialist Worker', claiming that the working class had been "Sold down the Mersey!"

Conversely, when the objective situation had become really difficult, if not mostly unfavourable, for revolutionary socialists, what did Tony Cliff, for decades the chief theoretician of the SWP, declare? The 1990s were, according to Cliff, "Like a rerun of the 1930s in slow motion." Truly a case of the celebrated fable in Russian literature of a fool singing a funeral dirge at a wedding and a wedding song at a funeral! This conclusion, moreover, was advanced by Cliff not just at the beginning of the 1990s, when it was not absolutely clear what the political repercussions of the collapse of the Berlin Wall would be, but throughout the decade and beyond. The 'nothing-has-changed' scenario painted by Cliff meant that the IST organisations, particularly the SWP in Britain, but not exclusively, could continue with fanatical zeal to organise and build their organisation – involving a rapid turnover of membership – on the premise of a radicalised period. With their advocacy of simplistic ideas and slogans such as, "One solution, Revolution!" they took no account, whatsoever, of the recession in the broad consciousness of the working class,

For a time, it was possible to sustain such an approach to building a movement but at a cost internally. There was an inevitable questioning within the SWP/IST's ranks when the false perspectives of this organisation clashed with the reality of the milieu within which their members worked. The consequence was an inevitable swing from sectarianism to opportunism, reinforced by the death of Cliff in 2001; and it was an extreme opportunist adaptation at that. Its manifestation in Britain is the tail-ending of left figures – or those who appear to stand on the left – such as Ken Livingstone, after his expulsion from the Labour Party and while he was campaigning to be Mayor of London in 2000. Livingstone has turned out to be a solid pillar of Blairism, which laid the basis for his return back to the Labour Party! Following his readmission, Livingstone's first preference vote, during the 2004 mayoral elections, while in absolute terms rising by over 17,600, on a larger turnout, fell in percentage terms from 39% to 34.5%. In June 2004, Livingstone shamefully stated that he would cross the picket lines of the London Underground workers because they would not bow to his diktats in wage negotiations.

The careful attempts of the England and Wales section of the CWI – the Socialist Party – to organise the original 'Socialist Alliance' as a holding organisation preparing the basis for a future new workers' party, was shattered by the entry of the SWP and the sectarian methods they employed. Up to their joining, the Socialist Alliance had been a genuine attempt for different, mostly small, organisations (with the exception of the Socialist Party) to carry out a limited united front tactic, primarily for electoral purposes. This all changed with the entry of the SWP. Using their weight of numbers, in London, in particular with their large petty bourgeois membership, and also their material resources, the SWP insisted on a single 'line' predetermined by them. This took the form of opposing others on the left, such as the anti-privatisation and RMT-backed, 'Campaign Against Tube Privatisation', in the Greater London Assembly elections of 2000, as well as other single-issue campaigns, which wished to come together with organisations on the left in a common electoral front.

Marxists in broad formations

Materially rich, the SWP is ideologically poverty-stricken, especially when it comes to elaborating the complex strategy and tactics needed to lay the foundations for new formations of the working class. The Socialist Party argued for a federal approach inside the Socialist Alliance, through which common understanding and mutual confidence could be developed, and genuine agreement on programme, etc. could be debated and arrived at. This was totally rejected by the SWP. They wished to impose their approach, their programme and their methods, none of which have proved to be successful in any serious struggles of the British working class.

This has not stopped the SWP leaders from acting like peacocks when pronouncing on the 'importance' of their party. This was shown by John Rees in his reply to Murray Smith (an ex-CWI member and now once more safely ensconced within the ranks of the USFI, which he originally left to join the CWI). In a debate over 'The Broad Party, the Revolutionary Party and the United Front', Rees states: "Murray Smith treats the development of the Socialist Workers' Party as if it were only tangentially related to the state of the class struggle when in fact that was the central, and publicly discussed, heart of the matter".[22]

In what way was the SWP "central"? Militant, the British section of the CWI, led two mass battles against the Thatcher government: in Liverpool between 1984 and 1987, and against the hated poll tax. In Liverpool, this involved solid industrial sections of the working class, who not only supported the central strategy and tactics, but rallied to Militant as a political organisation, which, at one stage, organised 1,000 members under its banner on Merseyside. During the British miners' strike (1984-85), we recruited 500 miners and had a significant effect in key areas of the NUM. During this period, the SWP denounced others who were leading struggles, sometimes in shrill denunciatory tones or, on other occasions, adopted a totally passive tone. For instance, in the anti-poll tax struggle, Tony Cliff, at a meeting in Scotland, infamously suggested that not paying the poll tax was similar to not paying your bus fare! The consequence of this was that the SWP played absolutely no role in the anti-poll tax struggle. They did not have a single member on the All-Britain Anti-Poll Tax Federation National Committee. But this did not stop them from claiming later, out of earshot of Militant supporters, both in Britain and internationally, that they were "really leading the campaign".

The consequence of this, as Rees admits, is that for virtually 20 years his organisation was hermetically sealed off from the real developments amongst the working class including setbacks. Instead, they were nourished on a diet of perpetual radicalisation, particularly in the 1990s which, as we have seen, just was not there. For a time, it is possible for an organisation based upon unstable petty bourgeois elements and not workers, to act out of consonance with objective reality and to yet grow. But it inevitably faces a day of reckoning when the internal political diet does not correspond to the daily reality confronting its members. In that situation, a party like the SWP can swing from the most ingrained sectarian methods, utterly repellent to workers and those on the left, to gross opportunism.

This is indicated on many issues: from the IST/SWP's stance on the Iraq War and their tactics in the 'Stop the War Committees' to, in Britain, most noticeably, their analysis of the Labour Party and its class character. By their own admission, the IST/SWP have swung from one position to another: "During the long boom, a small organisationally loose but ideologically clear propaganda group, the International Socialists (IS), was all it was possible to build," according to John Rees. He then claims: "In 1968 the IS grew. Over the subsequent years it gained a small but real working class implementation... it became a democratic centralist organisation... thus more open and agitational work, including the establishment of rank and file papers... went together with the more 'Leninist' form of party organisation."[23] What Rees is not prepared to admit is that this way of working inevitably brought them into collision with the few workers who entered their ranks; and who very quickly left. For instance, 'Rank and File Groups', in Leicester and elsewhere, were arbitrarily wound up by Cliff personally as soon as the miners showed the slightest independence from the leadership's line. Those who were involved in these groups were invited to join the SWP forthwith, with few responding positively to this offer.

Democracy and the party

The SWP has never been able to tolerate oppositions within their ranks. The CWI and Militant, which has been accused by the SWP and others of being 'monolithic', nevertheless experienced factional struggles, and allowed full rights for factions. This was the case before the small Ted Grant split of 1992, and also before the departure of the Sheridan-McCombes leadership of the Scottish section of the CWI in the late 1990s. No such possibilities were entertained for oppositions to exist within the ranks of the British SWP. They are invariably met with suspension and expulsion.

This was clearly the case with the expulsion of the US section of the IST, the International Socialist Organisation (ISO), in 2001. Political opposition to the IST leadership, based in London around the British SWP, was sufficient for the ISO (who claimed 1,000 members) to be expelled virtually in toto, leaving a small rump of IST loyalists. The same fate was meted out to those who sympathised with or supported the ISO, such as the majority of the Greek section.

In setting up the IST, Cliff claimed that this was not like other alleged "Trotskyist Internationals". It was more democratic, he said. There would be no international structures, no elections for international bodies or an international leadership. The task was to build national sections loosely bound together, it was claimed, under the umbrella of the IST. However, as the public disagreements between the SWP leadership and the ISO in the US demonstrated, this was a complete sham. The leadership of the British SWP decided the "line" and any opposition to this was invariably met with disciplinary action, without any recourse by those on the receiving end to discuss through democratic structures, or to appeals, or to the possibility of overturning decisions against them. In other words, this loose, apparently less "rigid" and, therefore, more "democratic" form of international organisation, was exactly the opposite. It allowed the leadership of the biggest section, the British SWP, to dictate policy, programme and organisation to the rest of the IST. You can build an organisation of "obedient fools" in this way but never an organisation of genuine co-thinkers and cadres who are capable of analysing and arriving at decisions independently - which is an indispensable quality for a genuine Marxist and revolutionary leadership.

The same methods were arbitrarily used by the SWP within the Socialist Alliance. This inevitably brought them into conflict with those organisations that remained after the departure in 2002 of the Socialist Party (CWI). Many of them were critical of our decision to leave but were ineluctably forced to tread in our footsteps as the methods of the SWP sharply clashed with the elementary democratic procedures of the united front or even basic collaborative efforts of those on the left.

Having served the SWP's purposes, the Socialist Alliance in Britain has been effectively wound up; the SWP have decided to put it at the service of the newly-formed 'Respect' coalition, which was largely a device for the European elections in Britain in 2004, around the figure of expelled Labour MP George Galloway. The expectation that this organisation could be the springboard for a new mass initiative, a step towards a pre- or actual new workers' party will be dashed because of the false methods and policies of Galloway's main movers of this project, the SWP. The sheer opportunist adaptation of the current phase of the SWP is demonstrated most clearly in relation to the Labour Party. Rees, for instance, claims: "Labour remains working class in the following crucial sense: its individual members are overwhelmingly working class."[24] Only a political formation that never experienced the Labour Party in a period when workers actually participated in it and, within limits, decided its policies and actions, could make such an incredible statement.

Working-class participation in the Labour Party is minimal and in many areas of Britain non-existent. We are not the only ones who claim this; Rees should read comments in the left Labour press such as Tribune, which regularly reports on the scorn with which Labour Party members and ex-members view the party today. Those who reluctantly cling to the Labour Party are predominantly the older generation for whom historical inertia – the lack of a real alternative, as well as the need to bar the way to an even more right-wing Tory party – is the main motivation for partic-ipating in and voting Labour. But this party has ceased to be working class in its base in the sense that we, and Marxists in general, understood it. In the past it really was a 'bourgeois workers' party' with a bourgeois or pro-bourgeois leadership but also with a working class base, particularly from the trade unions.

Bizarrely, the SWP now argues that those on the left and socialists who are still in the Labour Party should remain there. Yet Liz Davies, a former Labour left who collaborated with the SWP for a time in the Socialist Alliance, before she left the Alliance, protesting about the SWP's methods, stated in her letter of resignation: "In this report [of the 2002 SWP conference], SWP leaders are quoted as arguing that 'reformists' should remain inside the Labour Party – quite a different perspective from what was put to me by these same people when they asked me to join in 2001."

The current futile efforts of the trade union leaders in Britain to 'reclaim the Labour Party' will be stillborn. As one of the magnificent Liverpool 47 ex-councillors put it, in relation to Liverpool Labour Party: "Good luck to the left leaders if they want to try and reclaim the Labour Party, the problem however is to find it first." In its stand on the Labour Party, the SWP is to the right of the best militant fighters in the trade unions, such as in the railworkers' union, the RMT, and even its leadership, which has effectively disaffiliated in Scotland, and may do so in the rest of Britain. The Fire Brigades Union (FBU) has taken the same decision following a resolution moved by CWI members through the Northern Ireland FBU. This comes at a time when the SWP and their supporters muddy the waters. Rather than pose things clearly, suggesting disaffiliation from the pro-imperialist, rotten, ex-workers' party – the Labour Party – and to begin the task of constructing a new party, the SWP merely propose "democratisation" of the political funds of the unions.

The arguments of the SWP today are analogous to those deployed by misguided workers and conservative trade union leaders in the latter part of the nineteenth century, who argued that the working class should remain as a tail of the Liberal Party and "reclaim it"! The same arguments – "the theory of the lesser evil" – are deployed in the USA to justify support for the Democrats against Bush. This is vigorously opposed by the US supporters of the CWI who say: "This argument can be deployed not just for 2004, but for 2008, 2012 right up to 3016 if necessary." In other words, the theory of the "lesser evil" is an argument against the working class ever forming their own independent class alternative and ties them forever to the coat-tails of bourgeois parties.

The attempt of the SWP to equate illusions in 'reformism' (which undoubtedly exist amongst workers) with support for New Labour is bogus. In an era when the working class is subjected to vicious attacks from the bosses and their government, New Labour seeks to slash living standards. When socialism has been officially removed from the political agenda by the ideological campaign of the bourgeois, then it is inevitable there can be widespread illusions in a bygone age of reformism, i.e. incremental improvements in the standards of living of the working class. But how does this equate with New Labour? This party is a vehicle for vicious neo-liberal policies which seek to drive down living standards even further. The differences between New Labour, the Tories and now the Liberal Democrats, who accept widespread privatisation, are only of degree and, on paper, are very small ones at that.

Like so many self-proclaimed Marxists in previous historical periods, the SWP has adopted an increasingly opportunist right-wing stance in an attempt at a shortcut to gain significant political influence. This is not the first time, either, that they have employed such tactics; in the 1960s 'liberal phase' of this organisation, they opportunistically adapted to all sorts of episodic and single issue campaigns without attempting to skilfully link this to a socialist alternative. There is, however, some difference in their present stance, which is increasingly aimed at the tops of any movement and not to any radicalised base – i.e. George Galloway through Respect, Livingstone in the past, significant anti-war figures, etc.

Despite their ritualistic proclamations about the need for a 'revolutionary party', in practice the SWP is in a rapid evolution away from their previous aim. Like the leadership of the SSP, or of the LCR in France, this marks a significant departure from former positions. This could lead them to become the ideological, and to some extent the organisational, backbone of a sizeable, even mass, reformist, left reformist or even centrist current which could develop in the future on the basis of a sharpening economic or social crisis. While this may not result in a complete formal abandonment of their previous 'ideals', in practice, in the future, they will be relegated to the mists of time. Today, they downplay their former 'revolutionary' utterances, effectively sidelining their central 'socialist' message, in order to put forward a more 'radical' broad position which they believe is the only way to reach working class people.

There have been many periods in history when the ideas of socialism appear to have faded almost to extinction. The co-founder of scientific socialism, Friedrich Engels, commented that after the execution of Babeuf at the end of the French Revolution, his socialist and communist ideas were confined to the "back alleys" of Paris and other French cities. However, the embers of these ideas were fanned into a small flame and then roaring fires of working class action by changes in the objective situation and by the growth of the working class in France and elsewhere. The French working class, in the movements of 1830 and 1848, and the immortal Paris Commune of 1871, as well as the dramatic and revolutionary events of the twentieth century, witnessed the inexorable growth of the working class and, with it, the ideas of socialism. The same process has been at work in other countries although the pattern historically may be different.

The premature death of the working class and with it, the ideas of socialism, have been proclaimed on many occasions, including, as we have seen, by Alan Greenspan today. The Bolsheviks, under Lenin and Trotsky, in the period following the defeat of the first Russian Revolution of 1905-1907, faced a similar situation as that which Marxists have faced in the 1990s. The adherents of Lenin were reduced to a handful and he, as well as Trotsky, was forced to combat those opportunist ideas, even within the ranks of the Bolsheviks themselves. Lenin also fought against all manifestations of ultra-leftism, such as the boycott of the undemocratic Tsarist Duma – a policy that was initially adopted by the majority of the Bolsheviks following the defeat of the 1905-1907 Russian Revolution.

SWP's reformism

Reformism – a programme which restricts the workers' struggle to allegedly "achievable aims" and fosters the illusion that society can be transformed by incremental changes over a protracted period – was energetically combated by Marxists from the time of Marx. In the era of globalised capitalism, with its programme of brutal neo-liberal attacks on the working class, these ideas are more Utopian than they have ever been. This does not mean that Marxists must not fight in defence of every past gain or that they should not struggle for improvements in the conditions of the working class. However, we must constantly seek to explain that, even when victories are achieved, these of necessity are of a temporary character – given with the left hand and taken back by the right when conditions are 'ripe'. It is therefore necessary to build a powerful working class force that can carry through a socialist transformation in the organisation and running of society.

The forces of socialism and Marxism were thrown back in terms of numbers and support in the 1990s. But the viability of democratic and liberating socialism, as propounded by Marx, Engels, Lenin and Trotsky, retains its validity even in a period of relative isolation of the forces which argue for them. The march of events, the breakdown of capitalism, creates changes in the conditions and ultimately, therefore, in the consciousness of the working class. It can and will bring these ideas back onto the political agenda. That process is already under way, as explained earlier, and will develop at a ferocious pace, probably before the first decade of the 21st century is out. While fighting for socialism, the CWI is closely involved in the day-to-day struggles of working people.

Unlike others who are prepared just to comment from the sidelines, the CWI has never hesitated to get involved in the day-to-day struggles of the working class. Hence, our achievements in a number of countries. Our British section, a pioneer in many fields, as mentioned above, now has the most successful electoral record of any party to the left of the Labour Party in England and Wales. Moreover, in the trade unions we have a more significant number of members of the Socialist Party on national committees and at the base than any other trend on the left in Britain. This has only been possible because our trade union cadres and our members generally have dug roots in local areas and within some of the trade unions.

At the same time, we have never hidden our ideas and our programme, openly proclaiming ourselves as socialists and Trotskyists. More importantly, we have expressed the general ideas of Marxism in a manner that can be grasped by the most developed working men and women. This is why the CWI, in general, has managed to gather some of the best working class fighters into its ranks, although still too few for the tasks ahead.

The IST, exemplified by the SWP in Britain, is generally regarded with suspicion in the workers' movement internationally. In every major strike in Britain – be it the recent firefighters' dispute, the local government workers' strike, the struggle at Heathrow, etc. – whenever Socialist Party members visited picket lines, they were invariably met with the demand: "You are not members of the SWP, are you?" Only after assuring these workers that we were not, were our comrades able to get a hearing! The SWP's attitude was, in the past, accompanied with an extremely derogatory approach towards left leaders. They were denounced as "sell-outs" by the SWP in a most vicious sectarian fashion. This, of course, was during Cliff's 1990s period of "Back to the 1930s in slow motion". His hyperbole led the SWP to the ludicrous claim that if they had 15,000 members and 30,000 supporters on the mass miners' demonstration of 21 October 1992 – probably 100,000 people participated on this demonstration – the SWP could have led a march on Parliament, Tory MPs would not have dared to support Michael Heseltine's pit closures programme, and John Major's government would have collapsed![25]

As we have seen, with some delay, this clash with the reality of the 1990s has, in turn, led the SWP to swing through a 180° arc over their own heads to a total adaptation to left figures under a newly-discovered need for "unity of the left". This involves a political kow-towing to radical and left figures in the 'Stop the War Coalition', and in their latest front, Respect. They have done the same thing in trade union elections. For instance, in the teachers' union, the NUT, the SWP blocked with the non-socialist Campaign for a Democratic Fighting Union (CDFU) against the only serious left-wing candidate, Martin Powell-Davies. The SWP's zigzag in policy has inevitably created tensions in their ranks, which is a guarantee that the constant turnover in their membership – always a feature of this organisation – will be aggravated. This could also result in major splits.

As they have shifted towards the right, the SWP has also shifted in the direction of the USFI. They claim that the core of "The revolutionary left... comprises those Marxist organisations that managed to survive the defeats of the 1980s [?!] – most importantly on an international scale, supporters of the International Socialist

Tendency (IST) and the United Secretariat of the Fourth International (USFI)".[26] By this kind of sleight of hand, the IST hope to wipe out the CWI – excise it from the world political stage, with its considerable implantation in a number of key countries, which far exceeds that of the IST. Moreover, the IST is, in general, composed of radical petty bourgeois, particularly in Britain. The CWI's Socialist Party is numerically smaller than the SWP at the moment (although this was not the case in the 1980s). Nevertheless, the Socialist Party has a more significant position in the organisations of the working class and has had much more of an effect on the political consciousness of the working class and the labour movement.

'Morenoite' tendencies

Other Trotskyist currents were also initially unable to come to grips with the change in the situation in the 1990s. Some of them are remnants of the 'Morenoite' tradition based mainly in Latin America, which had, and still has, in a number of countries, a significant effect on the workers' movement. Tony Saunois, who has visited this organisation many times, sums up the views of the CWI on this organisation: "The forces from a Morenoite tradition, mainly those in the Liga Internacional de los Trabajadores (International Workers League – LIT) and a split from their International, the Unidad Internacional de los Trabajadores (International Workers' Unity – UIT), have in their ranks quite heroic workers and youth. Unfortunately, they have made a number of mistakes in analysis on the character of the present period. They did not face up to the reality of the objective conditions as they developed, particularly after the collapse of Stalinism. Some simply repeated quotes and slogans from Lenin and Trotsky without facing up to the real world situation or the current tasks facing the workers movement. This was especially revealed during the period of the collapse of Stalinism. Basing themselves on their 'Thesis of 1990', they initially saw the events of 1989-90 as part of a continuing international revolutionary wave! For a whole period they refused to recognise the nature of what was taking place in the Soviet Union and Eastern Europe and what the international repercussions of this would be.

"It was not until 1996 that they finally accepted that Russia was capitalist. Even in 1995 they argued that 'The downfall of the bureaucracies through revolutionary action of the masses was a highly positive development because it destroyed the Stalinist apparatus.'.[27] In the same year, their Brazilian party, the PSTU, simply stated: "The collapse of the world Stalinist apparatus is a strategic victory for the socialist workers' movement."

The UIT, which split from the LIT, accepted the idea of capitalist restoration earlier than the LIT, partly as a result of discussions with the CWI. A section of this grouping unfortunately moved in a more opportunist direction to deal with the new situation. Like the former CWI members in Scotland, they have now moved to build broader socialist formations at the expense of the building of an independent revolutionary party.

The majority of the UIT rejected this approach and in Brazil have a well-known MP, Babá, who has been expelled with three other MPs by Lula from the PT (Workers' Party) for opposing the government's neo-liberal attacks on the working class, such as the pension 'reform'. The CST (Brazilian section of the UIT) has played a prominent role in the formation of a new workers' party (P-SOL - Party of Socialism and Liberty), which can open up a new future for the Brazilian working class.

Another organisation is the Committee for a Marxist International (CMI), also known as the International Marxist Tendency – the Woods-Grant group that split in the early 1990s with small forces from the CWI. We have dealt with their ideas and their increasingly opportunist degeneration elsewhere.[28]

An International or a "post box"?

One vital issue for Marxists today is whether or not it is necessary to build revolutionary parties and the character of the parties which the working class will require in the struggle to overthrow capitalism and establish a socialist world. The planet is controlled by a handful of ruthless capitalists. Their governments are led by a resurgent US imperialism, which threatens the very existence of humankind and even the planet. The British Sunday newspaper, 'The Observer', has revealed the contents of a secret Pentagon document, which warns of massive environmental damage. Climate change, it says, could even result in a "Siberian winter" in Britain within 20 years from 2004, if the damage to the environment goes unchecked.

The war in Iraq shows the lengths to which the 'guiding' sections of the bourgeois – in the US and Britain, in particular, but supported by others including Italy and Spain – were prepared to go in order to capture the resources, particularly the oil reserves, of the second largest oil producer in the Middle East. The fact that the 'liberation' of Iraq is in reality a brutal occupation and is recoiling on them does not undermine our analysis about the assertive, brutal, methods of imperialism, in particular US imperialism, in the modern era. The US will soon, at the rate of expenditure it is now undertaking, spend on arms for alleged 'defence' as much as the whole of the rest of the world put together. This is against the obscene background of mass poverty and a worsening of the conditions of life in significant parts of the world, with the prospects of this getting even worse as long as capitalism and imperialism is maintained.

The centralisation of capital, not just within nations but on an international scale, and the collaboration between bourgeois governments against the demands of the working class – particularly to enforce the policies of neo-liberalism – all compel the working class to organise counter-measures. However, if they are inchoate, merely restricted to a 'movement', they will ultimately be defeated. The massive anti-capitalist, anti-war movements have shaken the ruling bourgeois circles worldwide to their foundations. But even splendid movements like these, without organisation, are not capable of stopping the drive to war, never mind overthrowing centralised capital. This has been quite clearly grasped by the significant layer of young people and workers who have participated in these movements. The idea, therefore, of a party and of an International can grow rapidly in this period. The question is: What kind of party? Also, what role will Marxists and Trotskyists play within such a development?

The leaders of the Scottish Socialist Party clearly drew the conclusion of the need for a broad party, with which we concurred. But, they accompanied this with the idea that the maintenance of the revolutionary core, which they previously belonged to, was no longer necessary. Opportunism – an adaptation to reformist, non-revolutionary ideas, particularly in a non-revolutionary period – never openly proclaims its abandonment of Marxism or Trotskyism. Bernstein, who revised Marx's ideas in a reformist direction, maintained he was defending Marx's concepts. So, our former comrades in Scotland still claim to maintain their "revolutionary credentials", while in practice they now pursue a reformist agenda.

We pointed out that, inevitably, they would opportunistically revise their programme, on the national question, in particular, and on the need for a revolutionary organisation. Unfortunately, our prognostications have been borne out and in a much shorter historical timescale than even we could have envisaged. From constituting themselves as the International Socialist Movement (ISM) within the SSP, the leaders of this trend, as we have seen, in effect proposed that it should be wound up. But this met resistance even from within their ranks, which has delayed the process. Nevertheless, the ISM is now a loose grouping of part of the leadership of the SSP. It has done little to check the opportunist slide of the leadership towards a more nationalist position (support for capitalist independence of Scotland), or for a 'Social Europe'. On the contrary, they have, if anything, reinforced this process.

A similar situation exists with the USFI – particularly with its largest section in France, the Ligue Communiste Revolutionaire (LCR). The LCR openly states that it is no longer a revolutionary organisation but is more akin to left social democracy, although containing within it "revolutionary wings". All of this has been done in the cause of chasing after cheap popularity and electoral success. These opportunist policies are combined with a most peculiar internal organisation, which diverges considerably from the norms of a revolutionary organisation based on democratic centralism. An extremely loose form of internal organisation now prevails in the LCR.

On an international plane, the same loose organisational conceptions exist. The USFI's World Congress document, 'The Role and Tasks of the Fourth International, new statutes adopted in 2003' states: "The IC [former International Executive

Committee of the USFI] must continue to play its role at the centre of gravity in an ongoing debate with counterposed positions. The debate is all the freer, inasmuch as the statutes codify an autonomy of national sections which no longer imposes any obligation to carry out the positions carried out by the IC majority. This is even more open given the presence, at the IC, of outside organisations that take part in our discussions, without any organisational commitments towards us." In other words, this International is merely a discussion club which imposes no organisational obligations to carry out policies arrived at through debate. How different is this from Lenin's description of the degenerated Second International as merely a "post-box" and not a very effective one at that? The USFI now exists as an organisation for the exchange of international documents, rather than an international centre to mobilise the advanced layer of workers and youth and through them the working class.

A genuine democratic, revolutionary International does not 'impose' decisions arrived at on an international level in a top-down, bureaucratic fashion. Unfortunately, the USFI did this in the past, as did other international organisations which stood under the broad banner of 'Trotskyism'. The methods of Gerry Healy and the Workers' Revolutionary Party, in Britain come to mind, as do the methods of James Cannon and Joseph Hansen, former leaders of the American SWP. In these cases, when the leaders failed to convince different sections of their 'International', they usually took disciplinary measures or imposed a decision without proper discussion and debate. This is in contrast to the methods of the early days of the Third International (Communist International – CI), under Lenin and Trotsky. The Third International involved mass parties, in the case of France, for instance, but carried out a dialogue and discussion over a considerable period of time before a national section was obliged to carry out any decision. For example, Trotsky, on behalf of the Communist International, polemicised with the French Communist Party (PCF) over almost two years on the issue of the 'United Front', which the PCF initially refused to accept. Only after considerable debate, and with majority support within the Communist International, did the Executive Committee of the CI then compel the PCF to carry out its decision. Not to have done so would have reduced the Communist International from a combat international organisation of the working class into a discussion club.

There are obligations in any organisation or party and, of necessity, discipline in any revolutionary party worthy of the name. There are no rights without duties, and no duties without rights. Full discussion and debate, and the arrival at decisions by a majority, are necessary but then the decisions have to be carried out in a disciplined fashion. This should be axiomatic for a revolutionary party but it is not for the USFI today. In the case of a broader federal, transitional organisation, such strict discipline is inappropriate. But for an organisation claiming to stand under the banner of Marxism and Trotskyism, amorphous and woolly forms of organisation defeat the whole object of preparing a mass force that is capable, together with the working class, of overthrowing capitalism and establishing socialism. The fact is that the USFI, as with the SSP leadership, have abandoned, and in a light-minded fashion, at that, conquests of the past, which is what the real concept of democratic centralism is, and replaced it with non-revolutionary, quasi-social democratic forms of organisation. The USFI puts their case succinctly: "In a new International, the Fourth International will be one current amongst others. It will definitely involve a certain continuity. But the major feature is a refoundation on a new programme whose renewal, obviously, will be carried through on the basis of a new social and ideological constellation".[29]

The reference to the "Fourth International" is to the USFI and not to other Trotskyist currents, like the CWI, which still subscribes to Trotsky's concept of a new, mass revolutionary International. In all the writings of the USFI and its leaders, one searches for criticism of the political opportunism of trends that once were Trotskyist, like the Democratic Socialist Party (DSP) in Australia, or others that claim to still stand under the banner of Trotskyism. But this, it seems, is just not a problem for the USFI. Historically, Marxism and Trotskyism has had to struggle not just against sectarianism and ultra-leftism, but also against opportunism, reformism, centrism and other ideological departures from the body of ideas handed down by Marx, Engels, Lenin and Trotsky. Yet today the USFI declares: "We have the conviction that it will be through a systematic collaboration with other radical, non-sectarian currents and, especially, with the new forces that the new parties and the new international will attract." [30]

Class collaborationism in Brazil

Where such an approach leads to is concretely expressed in the class collaborationism of the leaders of the Brazilian section of the USFI in relation to the Lula government. Given Lula's sharp shift towards the right, they have correctly concluded: "The leadership of the Brazilian Workers' Party, which for years had asserted the class struggle and the fight against neo-liberalism, is today implementing a neo-liberal policy required by the financial markets and the IMF", writes Francois Sabidel, a leading member of the LCR.[31] The same point is made in relation to the RC in Italy: "Another example is the turn of Fausto Bertinotti and the leadership of Rifondazione Comunista in Italy, which is preparing to discuss the perspective of coalition with the centre-left, that is with the forces of the Olive Tree and Romano Prodi, President of the very neo-liberal European Commission." [Ibid.] Since these lines were written, the RC has indeed agreed to a formal pact with the bourgeois forces of the 'Olive Tree'.

In the case of Brazil, Lula's government is so far to the right that the joke amongst the Brazilian left is that it is about to break with the IMF, "Because [the IMF] is too left wing"! The Lula government, as the Brazilian section of the CWI has pointed out, has attacked both teachers and civil servants – resulting in a demonstration of 30,000 workers from all over Brazil in June 2003. In 2004, the standard of living of those in work declined and real wages are expected to fall by 15 per cent. One of the greatest disappointments of the Brazilian masses has been on the issue of land. Only 13,000 families had been settled by the end of 2003, a far cry from the 60,000 settlements promised by Lula. Yet, the Minister of Agrarian Development, Miguel Rossetto, is none other than a member of the Brazilian section of the USFI, Democracia Socialista (DS), who has presided over this retreat while other members of the USFI's section have been expelled from the PT! Most prominent amongst the latter is Heloisa Helena, who is behind the formation of the new party, P-SOL ('Party of Socialism and Liberty'). This takes place at a time when the DS remains as a tendency of the PT, holds the position of Minister of Agrarian Development in the government, as mentioned previously, but also has had members who are political appointees (advisers) in the Ministry of Economics. Even the 'left' of the DS restricted their demands within the PT to the withdrawal of these advisers from the Economics Ministry and do not call for the resignation of the Minister of Agrarian Development. This was defeated by what now amounts to a right-wing majority in the DS. All of this is effectively ignored by the USFI leadership which is prepared to see a 'debate' but not to make sharp criticisms of its Brazilian members who, quite clearly, by serving in a bourgeois government, are betraying the interests of the Brazilian masses. How different is the behaviour of the USFI section in Brazil to the POUM in Spain who, as all Trotskyists know, played a fatal role in derailing the Spanish Revolution in the 1930s? However, the USFI is guilty in buttressing not a "left" government, like that which nominally existed in Spain at a certain stage in 1936, but an avowedly 'neo-liberal' former left party, which is now sustaining a right-wing government. However, Heloisa Helena launched, with three other MPs – Babá, João Fontes and Luciana Genro –and with the support of Socialismo Revolutionario (CWI in Brazil), a movement for a new party, precisely because no opposition within the PT is tolerated by Lula.

The same diplomatic silence is maintained by the USFI over the Rifondazione Comunista (PRC) in Italy. On the one side, as recently as the summer of 2003, at their World Congress, the USFI could welcome what they claim was the, "significant breakthrough represented by organisations like Rifondazione Comunista and the Scottish Socialist Party".[32] In the case of the PRC, it undoubtedly represented a significant breakthrough when it was founded, but that was in 1991! It has not realised the original hopes of those sections of the Italian working class who revolted against the opportunism of the leadership of the DS (formerly the Communist Party) because of its political degeneration. The PRC has zigzagged from left to not-so-left and during the last decade the USFI members within the PRC have formed part of the leadership faction. Now, with Bertinotti's opening to the right by his alliance with the Olive Tree, the USFI inside the PRC have tentatively come out in opposition. But this has been done in the most woolly, incoherent manner. They say, for example, that since the end of June 2003 there has been an, "Opening…for an alternative in posing the problematic of a new relation between the PRC and what has until now been the Olive Tree, projecting a programmatic alternative around content emerging from the reality of conflict and social opposition. This is not a programmatic relation between two subjects, but a relation between numerous partners, open to the movements in the forms that the movements themselves will decide to choose".[33]

Make what you will of this! But the USFI has done nothing to prepare the members of the PRC and, in particular, the inactive supporters of the PRC, for the likely movement towards the right by Bertinotti. On the contrary, they have acted as a prop to Bertinotti, which has been knocked away as the PRC shifts rightwards towards the Olive Tree. Due to the political vacuum in Italy, it is possible that, notwithstanding this rightward movement, the PRC could pick up electoral support. However, while the inert masses may give their support electorally to the PRC, the active workers who have looked towards it up until now will either oppose it or fall into inactivity, some even dropping out of the PRC. Its electoral support could go up while its membership base contracts. Indeed, there is some evidence that this is happening already. This does not mean that the chapter of the PRC is over but in its present rightward evolution it certainly will not be an attractive proposition for big sections of the youth, who are looking for a socialist and revolutionary alternative.

Revolutionary events impending

The role of a Trotskyist-Marxist leadership is to foresee events and trace them out, including examining the political weaknesses of parties, their programme and the method of their leadership. Inevitably, the leaders of these parties can move in a rightward direction unless checked by a conscious rank and file that is influenced by the Marxist alternative. By these criteria, the USFI has failed, and will continue to do so as long as it keeps on its present political trajectory. None of this means that the possibility of new mass parties of the working class, containing within them a revolutionary core, is off the agenda. Nor has the prospect of a new mass International, which was the perspective of the CWI from its inception, become less important. On the contrary, the conditions which led to the foundation of the CWI – the revolutionary events of 1968-76, and the emergence of a new combative generation – will be overtaken by the explosive events that impend in the first decade of this new century.

The first few years of this millennium have opened against a backdrop similar to that of the 20th Century. It is one of wars – the most devastating of which, so far, has been Iraq – the poisonous fumes of racism, economic dislocation and crisis. Yet there is also an unparalleled yearning on the part of the mass of the world's population for a society of plenty and peace, of social harmony, and of the liberation and development of the talents of all. Such a world is not possible under outmoded capitalism. Sooner or later, the mass of the world's people – beginning with the working class – will clearly see this.

But great social overturns – and the socialist one will be the greatest in world history – are prepared for by a courageous minority. They sum up this yearning for change in the form of a programme and in the form of a conscious socialist, Marxist and revolutionary party, and the organisation that goes with this. This is what the CWI stood for in 1974. This is as relevant and as "modern" today as it was 30 years ago!

In the age of capitalist globalisation, we see the emergence of an embryonic 'socialist globalisation', which can only be fully realised through a new revolutionary mass International. This will not entail a sterile sectarian struggle between small groups. It will require a battle of ideas before mass movements for the acquisition of clear ideological answers to the problems of the working class and encompassing all the tactical and organisational inferences that flow from this.

References

1. Remarks by Alan Greenspan at the Bundesbank Lecture 2004, Berlin 13 January 2004. From the 'Bank of International Settlements Review', March 2004.
2. Karl Marx & Fredrick Engels, The German Ideology.
3. *Ibid.* p.52.
4. Bob Woodward, 'The Agenda: Inside the Clinton White House', 1994.
5. International Viewpoint, October 2000.
6. Vercammen, 'The question of the party: Trotsky's weak point', International Viewpoint, October 2000.
7. Michael Lowy, International Viewpoint, October 2000.
8. *Ibid.*
9. *Ibid.*
10. See 'Cuba: Socialism and Democracy – Debates on the Revolution and Cuba Today', CWI Publications, 2000 or visit socialistworld.net
11. *Ibid.*
12. Karl Debbaut, 'France: Workers on the move', Socialism Today, June 2003. Can also be found at www.socialistworld.net/eng/2003/06/28france.html
13. International Viewpoint, November 2001.

14. 'At the heart of the anti-capitalist combat... Relaunch, opening, regroupment and repositioning' Francois Vercammen International Viewpoint 349 - May 2003
15. *Ibid.*
16. Ted Grant, The Unbroken Thread, June 1989.
17. Available on www.marxist.net
18. 'Which Way for Socialism?' 2001, available (in German) at www.sozialismus.info
19. First published in 'Sozialismus von unten' ('Socialism from below'), Number 2, November/December 1994.
20. Tony Cliff, Trotsky: The Darker the Night, the Brighter the Star, p. 300.
21. Alex Callinicos, The Anti-Capitalist Movement and the Revolutionary left, March 2001
22. 'International Socialist Journal', Winter, 2002.
23. *Ibid.*
24. *Ibid.*
25. 'The SWP and the Crisis of British Capitalism', 1992.
26. Alex Callinicos, The Anti-Capitalist Movement and the Revolutionary left, March 2001.
27. 'For the Re-building of the Fourth International – Joint Declaration of the LIT and the Workers' International' (published in English), December 1995.
28. See 'Revolutionary Socialists and the Venezuelan Revolution' at www.socialistworld.net and 'Militant's Real History', at www.marxist.net
29. 'At the heart of the anti-capitalist combat... Relaunch, opening, regroupment and repositioning' Francois Vercammen International Viewpoint 349 - May 2003
30. *Ibid.*
31. 'A New Force', International Viewpoint, February 2004.
32. 'Fourth International: A Congress of Optimism'. 2003.
33. Livio Maitan, International Viewpoint, September 2003.

History of the CWI
Introduction to
March 1998 Edition

The developing world economic crisis illustrates how the international market dominates the globe. This basic idea of socialism is the reason why all genuine socialist organisations and parties have seen themselves as integral parts of an international movement. While a start to creating a new society can be made in an individual country, once its working people have overthrown capitalism, building a fully socialist society is only possible when the world economy has been freed from capitalism's grip.

This is why from the 1840s onwards there have been different attempts to create an international workers' movement. Solidarity is an important part of internationalism, but not the only reason that socialists strive to build an international organisation. A workers' International should also be a political weapon in the fight against imperialism and for a socialist world.

At different times strong international workers' organisations were created but, for different reasons, collapsed. The Labour Party in Britain is part of the Socialist International, but this really ceased to be socialist when the majority of its leaders each supported their "own" ruling classes in the First World War. The Communist International, created in the wave of enthusiasm after the 1917 Russian revolution, decayed and then disappeared as Stalin's clique crushed democratic rights and the idea of an international struggle.

The Socialist Party is the British section of the Committee for a Workers' International. The CWI, founded in 1974, defends the tradition of Trotsky's struggle against Stalinism and to create a "World Party of Socialist Revolution", a Fourth International.

Today the CWI has members and supporters working in over 35 countries on every continent.

The CWI's programme and policies are democratically decided at a World Congress, made up of delegates from its national sections. This Congress elects an International Executive Committee (IEC) which decides policies in between the Congresses. The day-to-day work of the CWI is run by the International Secretariat (IS), elected by the IEC and based at the CWI's Centre, which currently is in London.

Peter Taaffe

Origins of the CWI

This is a general account of the development of the Committee for a Workers' International (CWI) over the last 24 years. It is based on a speech made by Peter Taaffe at a European School of the CWI in July 1997. Valuable comments were also made during the discussion by a number of comrades, some with a long history within the CWI. In particular, Arne Johansson from Sweden, Angela Bankert from Germany, Francois Bliki from Belgium and many others all made important additional points on the history of the CWI. As far as is possible in a short account, their comments have been incorporated into the text. This is by no means a full account of the work of the CWI over almost two and a half decades. A proper history is eagerly awaited. It is hoped a comrade will be able to undertake this task in the future.

Foundation, 1974

The CWI was founded at a meeting of 46 comrades from 12 countries in April 1974. This was not the beginning of international work by supporters of the British 'Militant' (now Socialist Party), who were the main initiators for the founding of the CWI. Many efforts were undertaken in the previous ten years to extend the influence of the ideas of the British Militant internationally. Even without a single international contact, Militant always proceeded from an international standpoint. An international is, first of all, ideas, a programme and a perspective. The general ideas are the lynchpin of any organisation. From this alone flows the type of organisation that is required. Therefore, the history of the CWI, as with the British Militant, is primarily a history of the ideas of this body, in contrast to the ideas advanced by other rival Marxist organisations, and also of ithe CWIs organisational practice.

The need for an international organisation flows from the very development of capitalism itself. The great historical merit of capitalism is that it developed the productive forces, of which the working class is the most important, and bound individual nations together through the world market. Internationalism, as Marx pointed out, flowed from the very situation created by capitalism, i.e. the creation of the world market and the world working class. This idea is even more important today in the period of globalisation. The linking together of companies, continents and different national economies on a world scale has been taken to an extent never even imagined by Marx, Engels, Lenin and Trotsky.

First International

The first attempt to set up an International was, of course, undertaken by Marx and Engels with the founding of the First International. Marx attempted to bring together in one international organisation the most advanced sections of the working class: French radicals, British trade unionists, and even the Russian anarchists. Great work was undertaken by the First International, culminating in the heroic Paris Commune. Engels pointed out that the International was "intellectually" responsible for the Commune although it had not "lifted a finger" to create it.

This first great attempt of the working class to establish its own state made the bourgeois tremble. They drowned the Commune in blood and conducted a witch-hunt against those who they held responsible, above all the leaders and adherents to the First International. But the defeat of the Paris Commune also coincided with an upturn in capitalism and a serious crisis within the First International, especially because of the role of the anarchists, led by Bakunin. Marx and Engels led a successful struggle against the ideas of anarchism but, alongside the disruptive activities of the anarchists, the upswing of world capitalism created reformist illusions in those like the British trade union leaders, which led to splits and divisions within the First International. Marx and Engels then drew the conclusion that the First International had done its job, had established the idea of internationalism and of an International in the consciousness of the working class. But they also concluded that, having exhausted this historical mission, it should be wound up after moving its offices to New York.

Second and Third Internationals

The period which followed saw the creation of mass parties of the working class. These parties were mostly influenced by the ideas of Marx and Engels. This process culminated in the foundation of the Second International in 1889. This organisation developed in a generally progressive phase of capitalism. Tens of thousands of working-class people were mobilised by these parties, attracted to the ideas of socialism and given a basic class education. But because of the objective conditions - the steady progress of capitalism in developing the productive forces - this led the leaders of the parties who adhered to the Second International to collaborate with the capitalists, seeking compromises, which became a way of life. In effect, a stratum rose above the working class, with catastrophic consequences, once capitalism's progressive phase had exhausted itself. This was clearly shown in the onset of the First World War. The overwhelming majority of the leaders of the parties of the Second International supported their own bourgeois in the bloody slaughter of the war.

The adherents to genuine internationalism were reduced to a handful. Some who may feel that the genuine internationalists today have been enormously weakened by the collapse of Stalinism and the ideological offensive of the bourgeoisie, should ponder the situation of Lenin, Trotsky, Connolly, MacLean, Liebknecht, Luxemburg and other genuine Marxists, in the First World War. At the Zimmerwald conference, which gathered together those who were opposed to the First World War, the joke was that the delegates could have fitted into two stagecoaches! Yet two years later the Russian revolution exploded, and within nine months of this, the Bolsheviks were in power and the first genuine workers' state had been established. This set in train the "ten days that shook the world".

Out of the Russian Revolution came the creation, in 1919, of the Third International. If anyone has any doubts of the effects of the Russian revolution, read John Dos Pasos's 'USA'. He gives many headlines from the US press about the Russian revolution. Not just the yellow press, whose editors dipped their pens in mad-dog saliva, but also the so-called "responsible and informed" journals of capitalism, like the New York Times, which carried headlines such as, "Lenin Assassinates Trotsky", or "Trotsky Kills Lenin". Even more lurid was the edition which claimed, "Trotsky Kills Lenin in Drunken Brawl". The Hungarian workers attempted to follow their Russian brothers and sisters, as did the German and Italian workers. In fact, the whole of the European working class was striving in this direction. It is not possible to go into detail on the causes of the Third International's degeneration. Trotsky traces this out in detail in 'Revolution Betrayed' and other works. The main causes were the isolation of the Russian revolution and the development of a privileged stratum which usurped political power. The defeat of the German revolution and the later betrayal of the German working class with the coming to power of Hitler consolidated the political counter-revolution carried out by the Stalinist elite.

Fourth International

The political collapse of the Third International led Trotsky to pose the need for a new Fourth International. But the founding conference did not take place until 1938. This was no accident. This step was based upon the perspective developed by Trotsky and the Trotskyist movement of a new world war. As a consequence, Trotsky envisaged a mighty revolutionary wave which would sweep across Western Europe. He was absolutely right in this, as the revolutionary events of 1944-47 demonstrated. This began with the Italian revolution of 1943-44 and was followed by the revolutionary events in France and other convulsions throughout Europe. But Trotsky could not have anticipated that Stalinism would come out of the war strengthened and that imperialism would be greatly weakened. As part of this process the Communist parties, which had participated and often led the struggle against Hitler, Mussolini and fascism, increased their mass support. Social democracy was also strengthened. The very power which had been vested in these organisations by an aroused working class allowed their leaders to save capitalism at this crucial historical juncture. Capitalist counter-revolution was carried through, not in an outright military or fascist form, but mainly by "democratic" means. Social democracy and Stalinism, and the mass parties, which based themselves on these ideas, saved capitalism in Western Europe in this period and, in effect, laid the political preconditions for the beginning of the upswing of world capitalism in the post-1945 situation.

After Trotsky

As with all Trotskyists, we trace our roots back to Trotsky. We in Britain came from the Workers' International League (WIL), set up in 1937, and the Revolutionary Communist Party (RCP), formed in 1944. We believe that the analysis of this party and its leaders, like Ted Grant, Jock Haston and co-thinkers, was more accurate than the perspectives of others. They anticipated the development of 'deformed workers' states' in Eastern Europe and China, in particular. The leadership of the 'Fourth International', Ernest Mandel, Michael Raptis (Pablo), Pierre Frank and others, believed that this phenomenon - the creation of deformed workers' states - was an impossibility. Faced with reality, however, they did a somersault. Then they went to the other extreme and Tito, in Yugoslavia, became for these leaders an "unconscious Trotskyist" as did Mao Zedong.

Of course, the leaders of the RCP made mistakes. There is no such thing as an infallible leadership. Ted Grant, for instance, originally characterised the regimes in Eastern Europe, such as Poland or Czechoslovakia, as "state capitalist". But he checked himself, re-examined the works of the great teachers, such as Marx, Engels, Lenin and Trotsky, and came out with a correct evaluation of these states. Tony Cliff, on the other hand, maintained the doctrine of state capitalism.

The leaders of the RCP also made the mistake, in our opinion, of entering the Labour Party in 1949-50. The majority, led by Grant and Haston, correctly argued that the conditions were not there for successful entry into the Labour Party. The Labour government of 1945 was actually carrying out reforms, the creation of the welfare state, etc, and there was the beginning of the world economic upswing. It would have been more correct to have remained as an independent party with the majority of the efforts of the Trotskyists, at that stage, directed towards industry. But the capitulation of Jock Haston led to the disintegration of the majority and, in effect, the capitulation of Ted Grant to the wrong policy of Gerry Healy for entry into the Labour Party. However, because of the beginning of the post-war boom, even a powerful Marxist organisation would have been undermined. The objective situation in this period and for the foreseeable future was favourable both for reformism and Stalinism.

USFI Congress 1965

My generation entered the scene at the end of the 1950s and early 1960s. I joined our organisation in 1960. We had a base amongst workers in Liverpool and there was also a base amongst a promising layer of students who joined our organisation at Sussex University. We were, at this stage, part of the United Secretariat of the Fourth International (USFI). We had been forced into a very unprincipled fusion with Mandel's organisation in Britain, the Internationalist Group, later the International Marxist Group (IMG), in mid-1964. The old, rather self-mocking, slogan of the Trotskyists at that time was, "unhappy with fusions, happy with splits". And sure enough within six months - towards the end of 1964 - because the amalgamation had taken place on an unprincipled basis, there was a split. In order to clarify the situation of a split organisation with two distinct groupings, Ted Grant and I attended the Congress of the USFI in 1965. Our arguments for continuing to be recognised as the only official British section of the USFI were rejected. This decision was in the tradition, unfortunately, of the leaders of this organisation who preferred pliant followers able to carry out their line, rather than genuine collaborators, even with serious political differences. Our tradition has always been to try and argue out differences politically. The tone for the USFI was set by the Socialist Workers' Party (SWP) in the United States. James Cannon was an able workers' leader but possessed certain Zinovievist, that is manoeuvrist, traits. An honest approach towards the different sections of the USFI was foreign to this leadership.

The Congress of the USFI took place in the Taunus Mountains, in Germany, in November/December 1965. We submitted alternative documents and amendments to those of the leadership. We had differences on the character of modern capitalism and economic perspectives. We maintained, I believe correctly, that Mandel's ideas were neo-Keynesian in content. We also differed with them on perspectives for the Common Market, as the European Union was called at that stage. The USFI leadership clearly thought that European capitalism was at the point of "take-off", that capitalism would be able to unify Europe. We also differed with them on the analysis of the colonial and semi-colonial world. We were in support of the national liberation struggle, even under bourgeois leadership, but, without in any way, giving a shadow of political support to the leadership of these movements. The US SWP, which was then part of the USFI leadership, believed that Castro was more or less carrying out the tasks of genuine Trotskyism at that stage. There was no need, according to the US SWP, for a political revolution in Cuba, i.e. the creation of soviets, the election of officials, the right of recall, etc. However, in the course of the conference deliberations we managed to extract from the leadership a difference between Mandel, on the one side, and the US SWP, on the other side, in relation to China and Mao Zedong. When we questioned Mandel about a formula in their document about the need for an "anti-bureaucratic movement" in China, he admitted that the US SWP believed that a political revolution was necessary but that Mandel, Maitan and Frank believed that it was not. In general, however, despite the fact that our documents were the only real opposition at the congress, our ideas were not addressed and hardly referred to.

Refuting our arguments, Mandel & Co. recognised two sympathising groups of the USFI in Britain, ourselves and the IMG. This was completely unprecedented in the history of the Trotskyist movement. While there are examples of an official section and sympathetic groups being accepted, there was no precedent for an official section to be de-recognised or put on a par with a "sympathising" group. This was a form of expulsion, moreover, one undertaken in an underhand and dishonest fashion. We decided that the time had arrived when we must turn our backs on this organisation and the squabbling sects who described themselves as "Trotskyist".

Out of the USFI

We tried to follow the advice of Marx and Engels to their followers in Germany in the 1870s. Writing to Babel, one of the leaders of what later became the mass Social Democratic Party of Germany, Engels commented, in 1873: "It is easy to pay too much attention to one's rival and to get into the habit of always thinking about him first. But both the General Association of German Workers and the Social Democratic Workers' Party together still only form a very small minority of the German working class. Our view, which we have found confirmed by long practice, is that the correct tactics and propaganda is not to draw away a few individuals and members here and there from one's opponent, but to work on the great mass which still remains apathetic. The primitive force of a single individual who we ourselves attracted from the crude mass is more than ten Lassallean renegades, who always bring the seeds of their false tendencies into the party with them." (The 'Lassalleans' were the followers of Ferdinand Lassalle, who founded the 'General Association of German Workers', in 1863.)

Marx commented earlier, in 1868: "The sects see the justification for its existence and its 'point of honour' - not in what it has *in common* [emphasised by Marx] with the class movement but in the particular shibboleth which distinguishes it from it."

We decided to face up in Britain, Germany, Ireland, Sweden and elsewhere to the task of reaching those workers, particularly young workers, who had an interest in left politics and could be won to a Marxist and Trotskyist position. There were many very good comrades in the small Trotskyist groups, many who were raw revolutionary material, but the opportunities of transforming them into rounded-out Marxists were squandered by the mistakes of the leadership of these groups.

Guerrillaism and the USFI

We had fundamental differences with the USFI's approach on the role of students in the revolution, and particularly on guerrillaism. Their position on guerrillaism resulted in the destruction of many potentially fine revolutionary fighters. It is not a question of ex post facto criticisms but, at the time when the USFI was engaged in sectarian adventures in Latin America and elsewhere, we polemicised against them. In January 1972, for instance, when it was revealed that there was a split between the mainly European sections of the USFI and the followers of the US SWP, we utilised the opportunity in party literature to explain our position to our comrades and to theoretically equip them against the ideas of Mandel and others.

The main proponent of guerrillaism, at least publicly, was Livio Maitan. We will give just a few quotes from a document, written in 1972, of our criticisms of his position:

"This short piece is to familiarise the comrades with the present evolution of the United Secretariat (USFI), the organisation which we were expelled from in 1965. Internal documents of (the USFI) have come into our possession, which reveal a split between the mainly European sections of the USFI and the followers of the American SWP. The issue around which both tendencies have polarised is that of guerrilla war (but it doesn't stop there) and the attitude which their organisation has taken towards it. This is of particular interest to our tendency as it was one of the questions which we attempted to raise at their 1965 World Conference and which was dealt with at length in our document of the Colonial Revolution presented to that Congress and rejected without discussion. (See our document on the Colonial Revolution and the Report of the Congress):

"Maitan gives a number of quotes from the great Marxist teachers. Marx, Engels, Lenin and Trotsky are transformed in Maitan's hands from the masters of scientific socialism into guerrilla romantics who anticipated Guevara, Debray and their ilk as proponents of the idea of peasant based guerrilla operations. Thus, in a reply to earlier SWP criticism, Maitan has torn out of context extracts from Engels, Marx and Lenin in order to demonstrate the validity of guerrilla war! He quotes, for example, from Engels's Introduction to Marx's Class Struggle in France, which refers to insurrection as an 'art'. Engels was dealing with the problems of a proletarian uprising in the cities! Where the great teachers of Marxism have supported guerrilla warfare, it has only been as an auxiliary to the movement of the working class in the cities. Maitan's attempt to utilise articles by Lenin on guerrilla war in 1906 are a complete distortion. He makes Lenin appear more as a theoretician of the Social

Revolutionaries, in looking towards guerrilla war and the peasant movement as the most important factor in the situation at that time, than of the Bolsheviks. In reality, the Bolshevik Party had fought a relentless theoretical battle against precisely these ideas, insisting on the prime role of the industrial proletariat, while giving every support to the peasant movements in the countryside and attempting to bring it under the influence of the proletariat.

"Trotsky elaborated this idea in his work on the Permanent Revolution and in numerous articles on the incapacity of the peasantry, because of its social position, its lack of cohesiveness, etc, to plan any independent role in the Revolution; either it supports the proletariat, as in the Russian Revolution, or the bourgeoisie.

"Lenin did support guerrilla war in 1906, as an auxiliary when he considered the Revolution was on the upswing. Later, when it was obvious that an ebb had set in, Lenin opposed the continuation of guerrilla war, as he did the faction of Boycottists amongst the Bolsheviks who opposed any participation in the Tsarist Duma and the possibility of even limited legal work. He would have condemned as a slander those who, because of these articles, would have accused him of propounding the theory of guerrilla war as outlined by Maitan.

"The position is even worse in the case of Trotsky: 'On the question more specifically of rural guerrilla warfare, Trotsky grasped the importance of armed peasant detachments in the Second Chinese Revolution.' (USFI International Information Bulletin, January 1968, page 13). The impression is given that Trotsky greeted the peasant guerrilla war in China enthusiastically and uncritically. In reality, as the following extracts from Trotsky will show, he warned that because of the predominantly peasant social basis of the Chinese 'Red' Army, it could come into collision with the proletariat if it defeated Chiang Kai-shek and entered the cities:

"It is one thing when the Communist Party, firmly resting upon the flower of the urban proletariat, strives through the workers to lead the peasant war. It is an altogether different thing when a few thousand or even tens of thousands of revolutionists assume the leadership of the peasant war and are in reality Communists or take the name without having serious support from the proletariat. This is precisely the situation in China. This acts to augment in the extreme, the danger of conflicts between the workers and the armed peasants... Isn't it possible that things may turn out so that all this capital will be directed at a certain moment against the workers?... The peasantry, even when armed, is incapable of conducting an independent policy." (Peasant War in China, September 1932)

"As we know, the 'Red' Army did shoot down those workers who rose in support of it in the cities. Because of the impasse of Chinese society, the Chinese Stalinists were able to use the peasant army to manoeuvre between the classes and construct a state in the image of Moscow.

"And as if it were written for today, Trotsky answered the 'guerrillaist' arguments...

when he remarked in passing: 'The Russian Narodniks ("Populists") used to accuse the Russian Marxists of "ignoring" the peasantry, of not carrying out work in the villages, etc. To this the Marxists replied: 'We will arouse and organise the advanced workers and through the workers we shall arouse the peasants.' Such in general, is the only conceivable road for the proletarian party.'

"Not once are these fundamental principles of Marxism posed, i.e. of the social role of the working class, organised in large scale industry, being the only class capable of developing the necessary cohesion and consciousness to carry through the tasks of socialist revolution.

"On the contrary, having bent to the mood of the rural guerrillaism reflected within their own ranks, it is only one step removed from hailing the latest outbreak of urban guerrilla war as a step forward: 'We also envisaged the possibility of essentially urban guerrilla warfare and armed struggle.' (USFI International Information Bulletin, page 17)

"One of the ideas fought for almost from the inception of the Marxist movement against the anarchists and terrorists has been that of mass action by the proletariat as the main lever for the social revolution. No self-sacrificing individual or small group armed with bomb and pistol, is able to bring about the downfall of the capitalist system. On the contrary, individual terror can bring down a wave of repression on the whole labour movement, as has been the case in a whole series of countries, of Latin America and of Quebec recently...

"Hansen, on behalf of the SWP in replying to the arguments of Maitan and Mandel, gives a crushing indictment of the present open 'guerrillaist' orientation of the majority in his own international organisation. Many correct points are made against the majority with which we would... agree.

"But Hansen's criticisms are at the same time levelled at the positions which he and the SWP held only yesterday and which they have not completely abandoned.

"Many of the ideas and even the formulations relating to the role of guerrilla war and by implication the peasantry are borrowed from our documents presented at the 1965 World Congress.

"If the SWP now claim that they have consistently held this position they would have to explain why they opposed our document presented to the World Congress where a clear Marxist perspective is given in relation to developments in the colonial and semi-colonial world. Ours was the only position which started out from the fundamental ideas of Marxism, the primacy of the working class and the need for the Marxist cadres to root themselves amongst the proletariat.

"In fact the pro-Castro and hence pro-guerrillaist orientation is one of the themes of Hansen's document. He quotes with approval the earlier reunification document in 1963 which founded the present United Secretariat: 'Guerrilla warfare under a leadership that becomes committed to carrying the revolution through to a conclusion, can play a decisive role in undermining and precipitating the downfall of a colonial and semi-colonial power. This is one of the main lessons to be drawn from experience since the end of the Second World War. It must be consciously incorporated into the strategy of building revolutionary Marxist parties in colonial countries'.

"There is no attempt, as we have done in our material, to first of all lay down the main strategy of Marxist tendencies in these countries of first concentrating the small forces available amongst the industrial workers while, of course, giving every assistance to armed action by the peasants and attempting to tie in these movements together with that of the organised workers. The 'experiences' referred to are those of Cuba, Algeria, etc, i.e. of the methods of rural guerrilla warfare...

"Perhaps the most pertinent point in all the documents is that made by Hansen against Maitan: 'One of the items in the evolution of comrade Maitan's thinking might have been the internal developments in the Italian section of the Fourth International at that time when, if I am informed correctly, the bulk of the youth were lost to a Maoist current'! (USFI International Information Bulletin, page 22)

"This statement alone is a complete vindication of the criticisms we made at the time of the 1965 Congress and in our document on The Sino-Soviet Dispute and the Colonial Revolution (written by Ted Grant). We warned them: 'No concessions can be made to the degenerate nationalism of all wings of Stalinism... Those comrades who dream of an "easier" approach are deluding themselves. Nor is it possible to imagine an opportunist approach on "current", "modern" lines will succeed, while the revolutionary approach is left for the bedroom.

'Why should any cadres in the Russian wing, or the Chinese wing, approach the Fourth International unless it has something to offer? What have we to offer at this stage except the theories of the masters, reinforced and enriched by the experience of the last decades?' (Colonial Revolution, pages 25-26)

"The pro-Chinese position of the whole of the USFI not only failed to win over sections of the CPs becoming critical of Moscow but on the contrary resulted in the going over of a section of the Italian USFI youth to Maoism! They preferred the real Maoists!"

This position of the USFI did untold damage in Latin America. It is no exaggeration to say that thousands, tens of thousands, of young people and workers in Argentina, Brazil, Bolivia and elsewhere, who were initially attracted to Trotskyism, were led into the blind alley of guerrillaism by the leaders of the USFI. They had a similar position of uncritical support for the Provisional IRA in Ireland. Needless to say, their position as political attorneys for different guerrillaist leaders did not result in any substantial gains for their organisation. On the contrary, as we see above, it led at a certain stage to the recruitment of potential supporters for Trotskyism to go over to these guerrillaist movements. The USFI destroyed many potentially important revolutionary fighters.

Towards New Layers and the Labour Party

We considered that our main task in the period of the 1970s and also later, was to turn decisively towards the proletariat, especially to the new layers. In Britain, as we have detailed in our book, 'The Rise of Militant', we concentrated our work in the Labour Party and, particularly, in the youth wing of the Labour Party. We had to skilfully adapt to this milieu but we never hid our ideas. Indeed, it became a standing joke amongst our opponents that a Militant supporter would immediately be recognised by the allegedly exaggerated hand movements but, above all, if they mentioned that they stood on the basis of the ideas of "Marx, Engels, Lenin and Trotsky". This did not stop our "Marxist" opponents, who were usually located outside the organised labour movement, from criticising us for "opportunism". While we gave critical support to the left, particularly the Benn movement in the 1980s, we always defended our own independent position.

Could the same be said for those "revolutionary purists" who did not sully their hands within the mass organisations of the working class? The followers of Mandel, in a number of countries, opportunistically cuddled up to different left reformists and in the process watered down their programme. No such criticism could be made of the supporters of Militant (now the Socialist Party) in Britain. We built a solid base amongst the youth, particularly in the Labour Party Young Socialists (LPYS). Ninety per cent of our efforts were concentrated in this field. It was not just the youth comrades, but the older comrades who participated and played a role in educating the new layer of youth who were moving towards Marxism. We won a majority in the LPYS in 1970, as we have explained elsewhere, later taking all the positions on the National Committee. This probably went a bit far but the LPYS NC members were actually elected at regional conferences. Experience had shown that unless the Marxists won the NC position in a region, the Labour Party bureaucracy would hamper, undermine and frustrate the attempts of the youth movement in that area to engage in any genuine mass work. In the future, however, where we are engaged in mass work, in general it would not be appropriate for us, even where we have an overwhelming majority, to take all the positions in the movement.

We were tolerated in the Labour Party at this stage. One of the reasons for this was the genuine rank-and-file democracy which existed in the party. Also we were energetic, most of the comrades were youth, had very good ideas, etc. A wing of the bureaucracy undoubtedly believed that the youthful supporters of Militant would, as previous generations had done, move to the right as they got older. However, these "Trotskyists" did grow up but, to the horror of the right wing, they continued to defend their ideas and some of them even became MPs. They were not the kind of MPs that the right and the bureaucracy had anticipated. The 1980s was a very successful period for the Marxists in Britain, as we have explained in 'The Rise of

Militant'. At one stage our membership rose to 8,000. Three MPs - all known Trotskyists - were elected and made a marvellous contribution to the struggles of the British working class.

Of course, the ruling class hated us and put enormous pressure on the Labour bureaucracy to weaken us and drive us out of the party. As is well known, a series of expulsions ensued in the 1980s and early 1990s. However, this did not prevent us from reaching out to workers who were engaged in struggle. Alongside of the Liverpool battle, we gained invaluable experience in leading the mass movement against the poll tax. We defeated this measure and, in the process, brought down Thatcher.

Painstaking Work

The development of the British section has always run alongside the growth of the CWI. But it would be a mistake to see the CWI as a mere adjunct of the work that we did in Britain. The CWI has a separate identity. It was impossible to replicate exactly the experience of the British Marxists in every country even in Western Europe. Painstaking discussions ensued with comrades in different countries in elaborating different and varying strategies and tactics to enhance the profile, numbers and effectiveness of the supporters and members of the CWI. As explained above, even when we were restricted to the small island of Britain, we always had an international outlook. We never took a purely British position but always proceeded from an international analysis, only then examining how the situation in Britain fitted in with this. We were always interested in international contacts. Many of the international contacts that we made appeared to be purely "accidental". But these "accidents" were related to the changes in the objective situation which was affecting the working class and their organisations.

Building the sections

Ireland

A dramatic growth in our international contacts was related, in the early part of the 1970s, to the big changes that were underway in the mass, traditional organisations of the working class. But the first extension of our influence came in Ireland. We recruited a young student in Britain who then went back to Northern Ireland on the eve of the explosive Civil Rights movement in the late 1960s. He, in turn, made contact with a new generation of youth, both Catholic and Protestant, around the Northern Ireland Labour Party in the city of Derry. I was invited to visit the North of Ireland in 1969. I arrived just a week before the explosive, almost revolutionary, events in Derry of August 1969. I was able to make contact and discuss with a number of young social-ists at that time: John Throne, Bernadette Devlin (now McAlliskey), the late Cathy Harkin, Gerry Lynch and many others. We built a very important position, at that stage, amongst both Catholic and Protestant youth through the Derry Young Socialists. Later on, through our work at Sussex University, we recruited Peter Hadden, who went back to Northern Ireland in the early 1970s, and has played a decisive role in our section in the North and throughout Ireland in this period. Following these discussions I travelled south and met a group of youth who were members of the Southern Ireland Labour Party in Dublin. Unfortunately, most of them who proclaimed to be Marxists were absolutely unfitted for the task of building a powerful Marxist organisation. Nevertheless our work in the North of Ireland did, later on, lead to the establishment of an important presence in the South with the recruitment of comrades who became leaders of the Irish section, such as Dermot Connolly and Joe Higgins, who is now a Socialist Party TD (member of Irish Parliament).

International Union of Socialist Youth

At this stage, we did not just work through the different youth organisations in Europe but also in the international organisation of the social democratic youth, the International Union of Socialist Youth (IUSY). We came up against a youthful but extremely hardened group of careerists who had been groomed as future leaders of the mass social democratic parties. Their main aim was to occupy the plush offices and limousines of ministers in future social democratic govern-ments. We represented a mortal threat to them. Compared to the Labour bureau-cracy in Britain, these creatures were a much more vicious breed. Nevertheless, our young comrades attended every meeting, no matter how daunting or boring the task in confronting these young careerists, in the hope of turning up useful potential socialist and revolutionary fighters.

This paid off in 1972 when two of our comrades, Peter Doyle and Andy Bevan, were sent to the conference of the Social Democratic Youth in Sweden. They met Arne Johansson and Anders Hjelm who were immediately recognised as kindred spirits of the British young socialists. Arne comments:

"The visit of the two representatives of the British Militant came just at the right time. There was a radicalisation amongst the social democratic youth in Sweden, with growing opposition towards the bureaucracy. At this stage we were part of a left faction within the Social Democratic Youth. We were well known, so much so that a social democratic bureaucrat even pointed out the British young socialists to us and said that our ideas were similar to theirs and that we should 'discuss with them'. This we did on the evening of the congress and found that we had a lot in common.

"We were concentrated in the city of Umeå in the north of Sweden, in a loose left/Marxist discussion group. Without a doubt, unless we would have met Militant at this time, this organisation would have completely disintegrated. We were not politically homogenous. Nor was it preordained that we would automatically join Militant or what became the CWI. In fact, the representatives of the USFI, in the form of Pierre Frank, made determined efforts to win us. He travelled to Umeå to address a meeting of our student group. I asked him if he knew of the British Militant. His riposte was short and brutal: 'They are completely impotent!'

"Roger Silverman, on behalf of the British Militant, visited Sweden, engaged in very thorough discussions with us and helped to consolidate us on the political positions of the British comrades. We took steps to organise a serious Marxist force but one which was very, very small at that stage. On the other hand, the Swedish Social Democratic Youth was a large organisation and the bureaucracy had learned from the experience of Britain. They, therefore, very quickly moved to expel us from the SSU but this did not mean we were completely debarred from the party - you could be expelled from the SSU while still retaining membership of the social democracy. Nevertheless, the "loose left" in Umeå and elsewhere disintegrated, although we won some very good comrades to our organisation.

"Undoubtedly, the 1970s was a difficult time for the Swedish Marxists and only by digging in and establishing firm roots, along with serious international contact, was it possible for us to survive this period. In effect, we could not pursue effective entry work as most of our forces were outside the SSU and, subsequently, outside the Social Democratic Party. In the creation of our organisation, we had to combat not just the ideas of reformism but the false ideas of the Mandelites in Sweden. Their attitude was that the revolutionary students were the new vanguard of the working class and they adopted an extremely sectarian attitude to anyone who did not agree with them. Only by correctly analysing the situation were we able to survive and to make serious progress in the course of the 1980s."

Germany

We had a similar, although different, situation in Germany. I had met a German comrade at the LPYS conference in 1971. He was soon recruited to our organisation and, in turn, attracted a layer of youth who travelled into our ranks. But if in Sweden we had arrived just in time, as Arne commented, this was not perhaps the case in Germany. Angela Bankert comments: "The CWI came a bit late to Germany. The radicalisation of the youth was well under way. This was reflected in the youth wing of the social democracy, the Jusos. Unfortunately, it was not genuine Marxism, in the form of our ideas and organisation, which successfully intervened in this situation, but Stalinist-influenced organisations."

In a different historical context of sharp crisis, of a revolutionary or pre-revolutionary situation, this position in Germany could have been fateful, as had been the case in the past in other countries. For instance, in Spain in the 1930s, the "Trotskyists" refused Trotsky's advice to enter the Spanish young socialists. But the Stalinists were not so "pure". They entered and won virtually the whole of the socialist youth which not only strengthened the Spanish Communist Party but resulted in the lost opportunity for Trotskyism to establish a mass base. The consequence was the isolation of the Trotskyists and the defeat of the Spanish revolution. Angela comments: "We intervened, with our very small forces at the beginning, just when this radical wave was beginning to recede. Nevertheless, there was a very keen audience for our ideas. At regional conferences of the Jusos and the party, with sometimes 300 people present, we could usually sell about 150 papers."

Belgium

The Belgian section of the CWI was founded in 1974, again by "accident". Roger Silverman was on his way back to Britain and missed the boat from Belgium to Britain and was, therefore, compelled to stay overnight. He looked up a contact from an LPYS conference and from this original introduction, a group of youth active within the Belgian social democracy came towards us and were eventually won over politically to our ideas.

François Bliki, who has participated in the Belgian section of the CWI almost since its inception, comments:

"If we would have been in touch with the CWI prior to the 1970s, it is no exaggeration to say that we would now be the largest section in the whole of the CWI, perhaps exceeding the numbers in the British section. There was tremendous turmoil within the workers' movement in the early 1970s. This was reflected in the social democracy, with the shift towards the left, particularly by the youth. The biggest Trotskyist current at that stage was around Ernest Mandel's organisation, which refused to involve itself in this struggle within the social democracy. We were very young and inexperienced but, nevertheless, we had a big impact right from the beginning. In 1986, we organised a mass movement of 26,000 students in 25 different towns in Belgium. It was organised under the name of our organisation because the Belgian Young Socialists would not let us use their name. We made significant gains through the work we conducted within the social democracy.

"From an historical point of view, this work was entirely justified. But, of course, conditions change. The split with the Grant group in 1992 was also felt in Belgium. This resulted in 32 comrades remaining with the majority and 30 with the minority. This minority merely repeated ideas from the past which were quite adequate for their time but had become completely outmoded by the change in the situation. Whereas they have stagnated, we have undergone a big growth. Now we have over

100[1] and they have 20, largely older, comrades with a stagnant membership.

"In 1995, there was a split from the Mandel group with the best of the comrades coming towards and joining our organisation. At that stage, the SI (the Belgian group linked to the British SWP) had 34 members. They actually approached the ex-Mandel group, led by a comrade who is now with us, but there was no question of him joining this organisation rather than us. Then in 1997, at a national meeting with 21 present, the London-based leadership of the SWP tried to impose their international "party line" (although not implemented in Britain) which meant that the members of the Belgian SI would have to enter and submerge themselves into the social democracy. This is against the background where the conditions for work within the social democracy no longer exist for a serious Marxist tendency. We approached them and had discussions with the 13 who voted against (it was a majority) and, subsequently, the majority of these comrades joined us. It was the comrades who left the Mandel group earlier, and who had been approached by the SI to join them, who now went and participated in persuading the Belgian SI to join our organisation."

April 1974 - CWI and Greece

By 1974 it was clear that the conditions were ripe to take the initiative in forming a properly structured international organisation. Big movements took place throughout Europe. The CWI was founded at a conference in London on 20/21 April 1974. Four days later, on 25 April, the Portuguese revolution exploded and we immediately intervened. Similar upheavals were to take place in Greece and Cyprus soon afterwards, and the Franco dictatorship was on its last legs in Spain.

The history of our International is one of ideas, of an attempt to work out the most effective strategy and tactics for the building of the forces of Marxism. With a small organisation it is always a question of concentrating all, or most, of your forces at the "point of attack". For us, at that stage - the early 1970s - that was clearly within the mass organisations which still retained the overwhelming support of the proletariat. In one case, Greece, we predicted the need to work in mass organisations even before they had been formally created. Almost as soon as the military junta had been overthrown in Greece in July 1974, our organisation outlined the perspective for the development of a mass socialist party. We argued that this inevitably arose from the situation following the overthrow of the junta that would open the floodgates for the mass participation in politics which would take a new form to that which existed prior to the military coup in 1967. The new generation, in particular, was looking for a revolutionary road but was repelled by the parties which still clung to Stalinism. We

---

1 - Since this was written the Belgium section of the CWI has doubled its membership and significantly increaced its influence amongst young people and the working class.

identified the figure who would probably lead such a party - Andreas Papandreou. He had evolved from the leader of the "left" in the liberal bourgeois party, the Centre Union, prior to the seizure of power by the colonels, into a radicalised socialistic opponent of the junta. And very quickly after he returned from exile, in September 1974, Papandreou took steps to organise a socialist party, PASOK, which rapidly attracted big layers of the youth and working class who were looking for a revolutionary alternative. Our ability to intervene in Greece arose from another "accidental" encounter with a Greek comrade in Britain. I happened to be speaking at an LPYS meeting in the west of London soon after the junta had seized power and a Greek comrade, a playwright who spoke little English, immediately identified us as 'Trotskyist'. This comrade participated in the fringes of our organisation over a period of years. When he returned to Greece in 1973, and tried to re-enter Britain he was excluded by the authorities. This rather repressive measure against him turned out to be very fortuitous for us. He was there when the junta was overthrown and immediately made contact with a group of Trotskyists who had played a heroic role in the struggle against the dictatorship. He urged us to visit Greece, which we did shortly afterwards. At the end of 1974, I was able to win this group and another group to the CWI. The first group was led by Nicos Redoundos. Nicos still plays a vital role in Xekinima, our Greek organisation. Also, as we have explained elsewhere, we won a very important group of young socialists in Cyprus. Comrades Doros and Andros remain in our organisation and still play an important role. From the original group who joined us, Andros is now active in the leadership of the Greek organisation. We were able to carry through the fusion of the two groups in Greece which, for a period, worked quite effectively. Unfortunately, this unity did not last but, nevertheless, our organisation rose, at one stage, to a membership of 750. Moreover, it played quite a decisive role in the developments of the left in PASOK over a very important historical period. Now PASOK, alongside many of the other traditional parties of Western Europe, is in the process of abandoning its class base and, therefore, the task in Greece is to work as an independent organisation.

Portuguese Revolution

The CWI, right from its inception, was extremely energetic in intervening in any serious workers' movement. For instance, as soon as the Portuguese revolution broke out, both Bob Labi and Roger Silverman were on the streets of Lisbon distributing material hailing the revolution and outlining the perspective of what we considered was the likely development of events. For us it was not just a question of correct ideas but of ideas linked to action and intervention. A similar and very successful approach was adopted in relation to Spain. We have outlined in 'The Rise of Militant' how we intervened in the Spanish situation. What is not generally realised is that there were many attempts to establish contact with Marxists and revolutionaries but they were not successful until we came across serious forces in 1974. Lynn Walsh, at a later stage, was also sent to see whether the CWI could make headway in Portugal. We then looked on any international contact, as we do today, as gold dust to be carefully nurtured and developed with the hope that this would lead on to much greater possibilities later on.

We called our international organisation the 'Committee for a Workers' International' for very good reasons. There were a number of "Internationals", all of whom maintained that they were "The" International. We did not want to go down this road. We, therefore, called ourselves a "Committee", for a future mass International. We used the word "Workers" because we wished to emphasise the central role of the proletariat, in contradistinction to others who based themselves on the peasantry, guerrillaist ideas or the students, as the "detonators" of the revolution.

Sri Lanka and India

And it was not just in Europe, where our main base was, that we began to have success. We had a very important Sri Lankan contact in London who was in touch with a big left opposition that was developing within the Lanka Sama Samaja Party (LSSP). This was the largest Trotskyist party in the world, with a great revolutionary tradition, but whose leadership had moved in an opportunist direction by joining the popular fronts with the Sri Lanka Freedom Party (SLFP) after 1964. Through this Sri Lankan comrade, we made contact with this organisation led by Siritunga Jayasuriya (Siri), Vasudeva Nanayakkara (Vasu), and Vickremabahu Karunaratne (Bahu). Accordingly, Ted Grant made a visit to Sri Lanka in 1976 which led to closer political relations with these comrades. He also made a visit to India to a much looser group of 'Marxists' who had come into contact with us. I subsequently visited Sri Lanka in 1977 and the tendency led by Siri, Vasu and Bahu was won to the CWI. They brought with them a significant group of workers numbering hundreds. In effect, all the best trade union leaders who were in the LSSP came over to this trend which constituted itself, after they were formally expelled from the LSSP, as the Nava Sama Samaja Party (NSSP).

I also made a visit to India with Bahu after I visited Sri Lanka in April 1977. The discussions that we had with a group of 'Marxists', based in Bangalore, proved to be completely abortive. This was a grouping of pseudo-intellectuals welded into their armchairs, contemplating their navels even more than Buddha himself. We immediately turned our backs on them but, fortunately, made contacts with members of the former Maoist mass Communist Party, the Communist Party of India (Marxist) - the CPI(M). From the contacts we made in these discussions with very good, active workers in the unions and the CPI(M), we established the first basis of our Indian organisation. Roger Silverman subsequently made many visits to India and at one stage lived for quite a long period of time in the sub-continent.

First International School

After two years of the CWI's existence we organised, in 1976, an International school in the city of Ulm in West Germany. We made spectacular efforts in Britain to get as many comrades as possible to this school. We bought an old battered bus to travel to the school. This ancient vehicle trundled through the European continent, much to the astonishment of the population of the different countries that it visited. Upon our return to Britain we promptly sold the bus. The gathering in Ulm was partly a school and partly a conference of the cadres that we had managed to assemble around the banner of the CWI. Apart from the countries mentioned earlier, there were many others in which we had loose contacts or groups that were moving towards the CWI. One such group was in Cyprus, of comrades who played a key role at the time of the Turkish invasion of the island in 1974. They played a quite heroic part in taking up arms against the Turkish invaders through the youth wing of the socialist party, EDEK.

Expelled from Social Democracy

While in Britain we had great latitude for work within the Labour Party through-out the 1970s and most of the 1980s, this was not at all the case with comrades in other countries. The social democratic bureaucracies in the countries of Western Europe had learnt from the experience of Britain. Very quickly in Sweden and Spain, our comrades, almost as soon as they formed distinct and significant groupings, were faced in the mid-1970s with a witch-hunt and expulsions. This did not prevent them from playing an important part in the struggles of the workers and the youth in their own countries. In Britain, we had successfully launched a school students' strike in 1985 against the establishment of slave labour through the YTS scheme, with 250,000 students coming out on strike. Basing themselves upon the experience in Britain, the Spanish section of the CWI organised a massive movement among school students involving strikes of millions of youth. They also did great work during the Gulf War at the beginning of the 1990s. Our German section and other sections did extremely useful work at this stage as well.

Emissaries Abroad

But we did not just send emissaries for the ideas of the CWI to Europe alone. We also made a determined intervention in Latin America. In the early 1980s we sent comrades such as Paulina Ramirez, her brother, Mattias and Tony Saunois to Chile. This involved great danger for these comrades as the Pinochet dictatorship was still in place. Great work was undertaken in Chile where the basis of the organisation which we have today was founded. We also sent a comrade from the Spanish section to work in Argentina, which was not as successful.

Also comrades from Britain, such as Clare Doyle and Dave Campbell, intervened in the former USSR in the extremely difficult conditions of the late 1980s and early 1990s to establish the basis of the organisation that we have there. Other comrades, like Steve Jolly, Robyn Hoyl and Paul True were sent to Australia, where again great work was undertaken. This is now bearing fruit with the very successful growth of our Australian organisation.

Our general policy had always been to work, where this was possible, in the mass organisations. After the initial assembling of the cadres, the task was then to develop viable sections of the CWI. But related to this was also the best method to develop the initial cadres and, alongside of this, the leadership of the different national organisations of the CWI. Leadership is something that is not easily acquired. It is an art which has to be learnt and inevitably involves mistakes, particularly from a young leadership. There is nothing wrong with this - in fact it is inevitable - particularly on tactical questions, but the important thing is to learn from mistakes.

International Campaigning

A vital component part of the development of the CWI was the successful organisation of international campaigns. On the issue of Spain, for instance, before we acquired the initial cadres, we conducted a campaign of solidarity with the Spanish workers in general but, in particular, with the underground socialist unions and party, the UGT and PSOE. At that stage, this party stood well to the left of the Labour Party in Britain and of social democracy in general. These campaigns were important not only because they allowed us to intervene in Spain but also brought towards us important figures from the trade unions in Britain. In our discussions with comrades from Lutte Ouvrière, who were present at the 1997 European School, we made the point that although we have worked, and very successfully, in the trade unions this is not the only way of winning workers. It is possible to win some very good workers, some of them leading shop stewards, on issues which are not immediately related to work in a particular factory or in industry in general. For instance, we won Bill Mullins, who was then one of the leading convenors in a factory of 12,000 car workers in Birmingham, not on a trade union issue but through the campaign of solidarity with the Spanish workers. After he was won to our organisation, we pursued very successful work in his factory on trade union issues. He subsequently played a key role not just in Birmingham and the West Midlands, but nationally in our trade union work and is presently our national industrial organiser.

Defending Our Comrades

In the 1980s also, with the growing importance of the different national sections of the CWI, we were involved in vital defence campaigns of comrades who had been arrested for their activity. In Israel/Palestine, comrade Mahmoud Masarwa was arrested and tortured, Femi Aborisade and other comrades in Nigeria were arrested, South African comrades were arrested and some of them imprisoned. We also were involved in the leadership of the general strike in Sri Lanka in 1980, which resulted in the victimisation of thousands of workers. We organised an effective solidarity campaign with these workers on an international scale.

Nigeria

All this work brought towards us some very important contacts. Some of them were won in the most peculiar and unlikely conditions. For instance, the present powerful position that we enjoy in Nigeria was made possible to some extent by our participation in a "Black Book Fair" in London. A Nigerian lecturer visiting London accidentally came across a number of our books and documents. He was very impressed with the ideas contained in them and took them back to Nigeria. This had a big effect on a group of Nigerian activists who considered themselves Marxists, some of whom were still under the influence of Stalinism but who had heard about Trotsky, and they approached us for discussions. Through this we won the position that we have in Nigeria at the present time.

South Africa

Similarly, in South Africa, a group of activists, some of them lawyers and intellectuals who participated in the first formation of independent black unions in 1973, came across our documents. This had a powerful effect on them and some of them gave up their jobs and flew to London, into exile, in order to have discussions with us. This, in turn, led to a very successful phase of intervention in the underground struggle in South Africa where our organisation was considered as a "tendency" of the African National Congress. Some of the material produced in their journal, Inqaba ya Basebenzi, had a powerful effect on the outlook of the militants who were fighting in the factories and in the struggle against the apartheid regime. This was subsequently confirmed in the early 1990s when the apartheid regime began to disintegrate. This also led to the South African comrades intervening in Zimbabwe which led to the foundation of our Zimbabwean section.

In the USA the visits of Sean O'Torain and the work of Alan Jones, who comes originally from Greece, resulted in the setting up of the US organisation.

Exhausting the Possibilities

Work in the mass organisations, it was clear, was virtually exhausted by the end of the 1980s. More and more, the work of our different national sections was taking place outside of these organisations. But, as happens very often in history, we did not draw all the necessary conclusions as early as we should have done. I have taken this point up in my book, The Rise of Militant, where I advance the idea that successful, independent work under our own banner could have been possible in Britain as early as 1985-86. The persecution of the Marxists and the further shift towards the right within the Labour Party had completely changed the situation. The process had begun whereby the British Labour Party more and more separated itself from its working class base. We organised mass meetings attended by 50,000 workers protesting against the expulsions of our comrades. But unfortunately, we did not offer a clear organisational as well as political alternative, at this stage. We asked people to join Militant, which we still described merely as a newspaper. We were not a party. The main thrust of our propaganda was against expulsions. The call to join a newspaper, rather than a party, was intangible in the consciousness of those who attended our meetings. Contrast our experience since we changed our name to Socialist Party in Britain to the situation which obtained then. Two hundred and twenty workers agreed to join the Socialist Party in Britain in the course of the 1997 general election. The fact that we are now called a party has had a decisive effect on our own ranks in making them conscious of the tasks which are posed but also in reaching out and winning workers who are looking for a party such as ours.

1992 – Independent Work

As is well known, in 1992 there was a split in Militant and the CWI. There is no time to go into all the issues involved in this split - we have done this elsewhere. But what is clear is that the small minority that split from our ranks were utterly incapable of facing up to the new period and the new tasks which were posed by developments in the late 1980s and early 1990s. The decision to conduct more independent work laid the basis for the successes of our organisations in the course of the 1990s. The initiative of setting up Youth against Racism in Europe (YRE) led to great success, which we have detailed in The Rise of Militant.

But alongside of the establishment of independent national sections we have, since 1994, launched the CWI as an open International. It would not have been possible to have done this successfully in the previous period. The baggage which we carried from our work within the mass organisations inevitably led to us concealing the true extent of our international organisation. The truth is that virtually everybody knew about the existence of the CWI which was often listed by the different labour bureaucracies in the "evidence" they amassed to carry through our expulsions. The bureaucracy knew about it, our opponents on the left, particularly the Stalinists, spoke openly about this. It was the working class, unfortunately, that did not have a full knowledge of the existence of the CWI. Now, as a more independent organisation, we have corrected this.

We have moved to establish more independent work and an independent international organisation at perhaps just the right historical moment. A huge vacuum now exists in the workers' movement. Just look at the Malmo meeting of the so-called Second International in 1997. This was a gathering of social democratic leaders and bankers who very often were one and the same thing. Significantly, the opposition to this meeting, in the streets around the conference, was organised by our Swedish section. There is no mass Stalinist International today, merely fragments of Stalinism - some of them quite important - scattered throughout the world. Unfortunately, the comrades of the USFI, at their Congress in 1995, in effect abandoned the idea of building, in this period, mass revolutionary Trotskyist parties or a mass revolutionary Trotskyist International. We believe also they have begun to abandon the idea of the party as a revolutionary, democratic centralist organisation. It is quite obvious that you cannot have a rigid centralism in any organisation today. But though we have to carefully examine terminology and change it where necessary, nevertheless the idea of a unified International, of revolutionary unity, is an idea which we must defend, as we must also defend and develop the idea of the need to create parties to ensure the victory of the working class.

On another level, the Liverpool Dockers' strike in Britain[2] shows the need for international action of the working class like never before in history. The 1995 Danish bus workers' struggle also demonstrated the need for the working class to link up on the trade union level internationally as did that of their Indian counterparts in Bangalore. At the same time there is a greater need today, as I mentioned earlier, in the era of globalisation, to not only adopt a general internationalist stance but also to create mass political organisations which are linked together through a real mass International.

---

2 - This heroic struggle took place over a year (1996-1997) and evoked tremendous solidarity and support from working people in Britain and internationally. Unfortunately, the strike was defeated. The dockers remain sacked. Once more the right-wing trade union leaders, in particular, the general secretary of the dockers' union, the Transport and General Workers' Union, completely failed to organise the necessary solidarity to ensure victory.

Reassembling Revolutionary Forces

The question is how to build such a mass International. We have a vital role to play in this process. We have in the past, as I described, sent comrades to different countries and continents throughout the world to establish the first forces of genuine Marxists. If necessary we will continue to do this. But a new mass International will not develop in a linear fashion. The process will involve fusions, splits and the reassembling of genuine revolutionary forces on an international and national plane.

We have been very successful in this regard. From the beginning we managed to absorb into our ranks organisations that did not agree with everything that the CWI stood for. In Cyprus, for instance, the group mentioned earlier that eventually joined us, after quite lengthy discussions, was somewhat heterogeneous. Many of those who remained with the CWI and who played a key role in building a very important section in Cyprus were, from the outset, committed to the general perspectives and programme of the CWI. But there were others who could be described as occupying a left centrist position, vacillating between the ideas of the CWI and centrist ideas. Some of them dropped by the wayside as the group became more serious, while others evolved into genuine revolutionaries with a rounded-out outlook. Similar developments took place in Sri Lanka. While the NSSP affiliated to the CWI, the leaders of this organisation, particularly Bahu, never fully agreed with the analysis that we had made of Stalinism, of developments in the former colonial and semi-colonial world and the national question, etc. While successful collaboration ensued for a period, the differences never disappeared and were a factor in the split of the NSSP from the CWI in 1989 (although a very important minority led by Siri stayed with the CWI).

A more recent example of a fusion was in France.[3]

Renaud from Gauche Révolutionnaire (GR), the French section of the CWI, commented:

"We came to the CWI from the USFI. We had come into political opposition to the leadership of the organisation in France, the Ligue Communiste Révolutionnaire (LCR). From 1987 they had been pursuing a policy of "automation". They interpreted

---

3 - Murray Smith, who was instrumental in leading the GR into the CWI, subsequently returned to the LCR and was rewarded with a position on the organisation's National Committee. This is ironical, given Murray Smith's earlier criticism of another comrade's return to the LCR. Murray Smith said this comrade, "ended up badly"! However, Murray Smith has never been noted for his consistency. He was at one with the USFI in its support for the IRA. He admitted to me [Peter Taaffe], when he joined the CWI, that he was the author of the USFI's slogan, "Victory to the IRA", which they used in Britain. Later Murray Smith became convinced of the CWI's analysis and slogans regarding Northern Ireland, but who knows what his position is now, let alone in the future!

this to mean that every initiative undertaken by themselves was deemed 'sectarian'. Leading comrades of the LCR would even argue that to sell the paper was sectarian. The line was that we should try to intervene in 'new kinds' of organisational forms, new formations, for example, the developments on the environment and amongst the ecologists.

"There were, of course, some correct points in what they said. We have never hesitated to aid any group of workers in the labour movement, particularly those evolving towards the left, environmentalists involved in serious struggle, etc. But the problem with the USFI's position was that they never tried to put forward their own political line, but tended to adapt their programme, in an opportunist fashion, to the leaders of these 'new formations'. For example, when a left group within the Socialist Party (PS) launched a school students' union the USFI deliberately played down their own role and forswore any attempt to win this group over. At every demonstration, they lent them (the PS) megaphones, etc, because this group, according to the USFI, should be the 'leaders' of the school students' union. In reality, the Mandelite youth organisation was bigger than this group. This role of merely 'helping' the leaders of the traditional left organisations and not politically challenging them we opposed.

"In the beginning it was not clear in our heads but we wanted to build the forces of Trotskyism in an open, fighting organisation. We wanted to build and recruit to our party with our programme. Our clash with the Mandelites on this issue is what shaped our tendency inside their organisation. We had already begun to bring a newspaper out whilst still within the LCR. We won a majority of the Jeunesse Communiste Révolutionnaire (JCR - the LCR's youth organisation) in 1989. But you will see there have been many changes in our political line as we have sought to clarify our position. In the French Mandelite organisation there are several tendencies, which are really factions. In fact, the LCR is not a party but a federation of factions.

"They expelled us in October 1992 when we were quite well organised with a group of 50-60 young people around us. When we were expelled we were approached by many groups. I think comrades would be astonished at the number of Trotskyist groups throughout the world, many of them very strange to say the least. We know, we met them all. We had heard of the Militant, and at first thought it was a kind of left, social democratic, 'workerist' tendency within the social democratic and labour movement. But then we went through the experience of the Brussels demonstration after a comrade had seen a poster in Ireland.

"After the demo we approached the CWI with a view to launching the YRE in France. We originally thought that we would have to join the CWI as a condition for us setting up the YRE. But we were pleasantly surprised that this was not the case and that we were given permission to form the YRE. We thought that this was a very good start, which then led to political discussions and eventually a large level of agreement which resulted in us joining the CWI."

Murray Smith was also one of the founders of GR in France and, at the time he made the following comments, was a member of our International Secretariat. Murray adds:

"The USFI and Mandel had completely failed to understand the changes in the world situation. We had definitely drawn the conclusion that this organisation was impossible to reform after their congress in 1991. So, as Renaud has commented, we started looking around for other organisations. We did not confine ourselves to that but also began to develop our own ideas in opposition to the LCR. This led us to contact with many organisations, more than we wanted to!

"A comrade from the JCR who is no longer with us - he ended up badly, going back to the LCR - went on holiday to Ireland in the summer of 1992 and bought a copy of Irish Militant in a newsagents. This is how we came to learn about the October 1992, anti-racist YRE demonstration. In fact, we had been arguing for years within the LCR and USFI for them to take such an initiative. Following the Brussels demonstration we had many discussions with the CWI.

"What did these discussions actually amount to? We first of all had to get rid of any misconceptions that we were dealing with 'left reformists'. When you approach an organisation, you have to ascertain the nature of that organisation. Are these people Marxists? Are they reformists? Are they sectarian? Are they Stalinists? The second point is how do these people analyse what is going on in the world? What are their perspectives? And, of course, vitally, are they competent in building viable organisations both on a national and international scale? Through discussions we became convinced that both the Militant and the CWI met the criteria that we had set ourselves.

"There are many lessons in relation to how we joined the CWI which will be useful in similar experiences in the future. I don't think that fusion with other groups is the main way of building the International. I think we will build out of the new layers coming into action but, also, the question of working with other groups and fusion can be posed as well.

"In France, at the moment, there is a certain flux on the left. In my opinion there is the beginning of a break-up of the three largest Trotskyist groups - which were set up in the 1960s - with the emergence of an opposition in Lutte Ouvrière, for example. And at the same time, there is the emergence now of defined political currents, even with their own newspapers, within the PCF (French Communist Party). There is, therefore, the possibility of fusions and regroupments posing further questions for our intervention in the mass organisations. I think similar questions will be posed elsewhere. Renaud said at the end of his contribution that when we joined the CWI we weren't perfect - we're still not perfect. I think we have learnt a lot from the International and I also hope that we have contributed to the International.

"Just a word on work within the traditional organisations in the past. The French section is one of the few in the International which has never actually done entry work. We came into the International after the CWI had exhausted the tactic of work within the mass traditional organisations. I wonder if we had come in ten or fifteen years before, what we would we have done in France? Let's put the question another way. Could the LCR with 1,500 members, in 1968, and 3-4,000, in the mid-1970s, have been more effective in working within one of the two major mass organisations of the French working class? Hundreds of workers joined the French Communist Party in the decade after 1968 and tens of thousands joined the Socialist Party. Now, if the LCR had decided to employ the tactic of the CWI (given the size of the LCR) to enter the PCF - difficult but not impossible - or go into the PS - easier but not so profitable - is it not possible they would have made a much bigger impact? It seems to me that when an organisation of this size - and from that point of view size is important - could have maintained an independent organisation and yet, at the same time, worked within either wing of the mass organisations, that could have been the most effective method."

Lessons from the Past - for the Future

The main forces for the CWI will come from new layers of the proletariat who have only just begun to move into action or have not yet entered the political arena. The task of winning these layers may appear to be immediately more arduous than the "easier" task of trying to group together different "revolutionary" organisations. There are, of course, some very good comrades in different organisations with a different tradition to our own. It would be a mistake not to seek principled revolutionary unity with genuine forces. However, we have to turn our back on the sectarian fragments who will never be capable of building genuine mass Marxist forces.

The early 1990s were not the easiest of times for us or for revolutionary Marxists in general. But we managed to keep alive the revolutionary thread. We have analysed, we believe in a correct, rounded-out fashion, the objective situation which confronted us and the working class, and are prepared for a new, more favourable position for our organisation. While we are not completely out of the woods yet, the most difficult period is perhaps behind us. This does not mean that we will not have more problems but, at the same time, there will be great opportunities for the development of our organisations and the CWI if we work correctly. The achievements in the future will far surpass what we have done in the past. We must raise the level of all comrades, from the leadership to the newest comrades. Every member has a vital role to play in the development of the revolutionary movement. Each comrade, as Trotsky commented, carries a particle of history on their shoulders. We stand in the best revolutionary traditions of Marx, Engels, Lenin and Trotsky and the achievements of the revolutionary movement of the last four or five decades. One worker today can win 10, 50, 100 tomorrow and prepare the ground for the development of new mass workers' parties and a new mass workers' International.

We must learn the lessons of the past. There have been enough defeats of the proletariat. Because we have not yet attained mass influence, there are bound to be setbacks and defeats. But there are going to be victories as well. And in defeats and in victories, this new generation will learn the lessons of the past and build an organisation which, this time, will carry the working class to victory.

A meeting of the Sri Lankan CWI section.

Founding conference of the Democratic Socialist Movement in Nigeria
- now the second largest section of the CWI.

Postscript
Building the CWI
(1998-2004)

I n the years following the first publication of the 'History of the CWI', the sections and supporters of the CWI were involved in an even more hectic pace of activity. It is not possible, in the space provided here, to give a detailed account of the activities of the CWI and its sections, but a summary of the main areas of work will show the CWI's wide scope and important influence.

Anti-globalisation and anti-war movement

A s well as an upturn in class struggles in many countries, recent years were marked by the growth of the anti-globalisation and anti-capitalist movement and, of course, the huge protest movement against the Iraq war and the imperialist occupation of Iraq. The CWI analysed these processes, and the world situation following the S11 attacks in New York and Bush's aggressive imperialist policies, providing clarity to CWI members and supporters in times of a great sharpening of politics. The CWI rejected the widespread pessimism of many on the left, who saw only an 'unstoppable' imperialist machine. On the contrary, we argued that US led military invasions would only make the world more unstable and dangerous and that it would mean creating new problems for imperialism. In fact, the CWI warned months beforehand that Iraq would become a morass for the US and other occupation forces, and their presence in the country would lead to widespread Iraqi resistance.

The broad anti-globalisation movement represented a radicalisation of young people, in protest against many of the results of capitalist globalisation. This process – a political re-awakening after the setbacks of the 1990s – was predicted by the CWI during the last decade (when many on the left internationally had given up on the ability of youth and the working class to change society). It marks a step towards a general upturn in class struggles. Of course, this process is still at an early stage. But the anti-globalisation movement, and anti-war protests, did include those attracted to the ideas of genuine socialism, as the only viable alternative to the capitalist system.

The CWI participated in the anti-globalisation protests, including in London, Seattle, Prague, Melbourne, Gothenburg and Genoa, and put forward a socialist programme. In many cases, CWI members played a vital role in organising and running these protests. We also found an enthusiastic reception to the CWI's ideas during the World Social Forum gatherings in Porto Alegre, in Brazil, and Mumbai, in India. To participate successfully, meant combining CWI forces in Brazil (2002 and 2003) and in India (2004) with several other CWI sections – a practical illustration of socialist internationalism.

Undoubtedly, the broad anti-globalisation mood aided the development of the anti-war protests and debates, which started with the demonstrations in 1998 against the NATO powers' war against Serbia, followed by the protests in 2001/2002 against the US-led invasion of Afghanistan and, of course, the enormous demonstrations in opposition to war on Iraq, in 2003. The CWI sections played a crucial role in these protests, in many countries. Members helped to initiate 'Youth against War' in several countries in Europe, in North America, Australia and elsewhere, which held high profile school strikes on the outbreak of the war. Around 200,000 students marched throughout Germany. Thousands came out from schools in London. In Northern Ireland, Youth against War brought out thousands of Catholic and Protestant school students. The CWI in the US, Socialist Alternative, helped hold university college protests, as part of a magnificent spread of protests across the country.

Industrial struggles

The last several years also saw a rise in industrial struggles, especially in Europe. Most of these struggles were defensive and in opposition to government cuts. CWI members in England, Wales, Scotland, and Northern Ireland, played an important role in aiding the fire fighters' strike during 2002. Through this, the CWI increased its influence in this important union. Leaders of the FBU, the fire fighters' union, joined the Socialist Party in Northern Ireland.

The German section of the CWI, against the wishes of the trade union leaders, was instrumental in campaigning successfully for mass protests against Schroeder's huge attacks on workers. This led to huge demonstrations on 1 November 2003 and since.

In 2003, French CWI members are active in the teachers' union, and played a leading role in the worker's offensive against the cuts package of Prime Minister Raffarin. The 2003 strike wave in Austria provided a boost to the 'Platform for Fighting and Democratic Trade Unions', a network of union activists, initiated by CWI members, which resists cuts and the block of the right wing union leaders.

CWI members are also involved in important offensive struggles to win better conditions and rights, such as the successful classroom assistants' dispute in Northern Ireland for better wages, and the recent nursery nurses' dispute in Scotland.

The CWI now has an important influence in several unions in Britain and in Ireland. Eighteen CWI members sit on the national executives of British-based unions. Janice Godridge, the President of the PCS, a public employees' union, is a CWI member, as is Chris Baugh, the Assistant General Secretary of PCS, the main civil servants' union.

The President of the main public sector union in Northern Ireland, NIPSA, is Carmel Gates, a CWI member, and other Socialist Party members sit on NIPSA leadership body. For a period, the Socialist Party in Ireland also held the position of President of the CWU (communications workers' union) in Southern Ireland.

Union activity is also crucial for the CWI in the neo-colonial world, from Chile to Kashmir. CWI members play an important role, for example, in the teachers' union in Brazil, and are involved in the re-assembling of independent workers' organisations in the very difficult circumstances of the former Soviet Union (including in Russia and Kazakhstan).

Anti-racist campaigns

It is not only in 'Third World' conditions that a fight to construct workers' organisations, for basic union rights and for an end to low pay needs to be conducted. In June 2004, in Australia, a young workers' rights campaign, 'Unite!', set up by CWI members, successfully forced the management of a store of the multinational 'Borders' book shops to agree to improve the conditions of its young workers.

Both in words and in deeds, the CWI stands on the side of women, youth and the poor, and, in particular, oppressed minorities. Successful work amongst immigrants by the Greek section of the CWI has resulted in many immigrant activists joining the party. Sozialistische Linkspartie, the CWI in Austria, was to the forefront of the 'resistance movement' in 2001, which protested against the inclusion of the populist right, FPO ('Freedom Party'), in a national coalition government.

Australian comrades were instrumental in the campaign against the harsh and inhumane anti-immigrant policies of the John Howard Liberal government. This included helping to organise high profile protests outside desert detention centres. The Socialist Party (England and Wales), and 'Youth against Racism in Europe' (YRE), consistently campaigns against anti-immigrant policies of the New Labour government and also against the racist far right and populist right. The 'Blocbuster' campaign in Belgium, initiated by the CWI, was to the fore in protests against the populist, far right, Vlaams Blok. The Dutch CWI, Offensief, organised lively contingents, in 2004, during the large protest demonstrations against the plans of the right-wing coalition government in Netherlands to forcibly 'return' thousands of refugees to war zones, extreme poverty, torture and even death.

Working with other left forces

As well as building its own forces, the CWI is prepared to work with other left organisations, including in elections, where this is possible and in the interests of working people. During the June 2004 local elections in Germany, a member of the CWI, Sozialistische Alternative (SAV), won a seat in Rostock, standing as part of a left election list that included non-SAV members. Sozialistische Alternative is also currently working in the association, 'Electoral alternative for Work and Social Justice', which aims to become a new party. Sozialistische Alternative members will campaign for it to take on flesh by putting forward a socialist alternative to the SPD.

In Brazil, the CWI section was part of the PT (Workers' Party) but left this party, after it assumed power and carried out neo-liberal attacks on the working class. The Brazilian CWI is currently collaborating with other left forces in the newly established P-SOL ('Party of Socialism and Liberty') with the aim of creating a mass socialist and Trotskyist alternative to Lula's PT.

In Scotland, the Netherlands and Portugal, the CWI participates in broad left formations, while upholding the banner of Marxism. Following the departure of former CWI members in Scotland, in 2000, to form the majority of the leadership of the Scottish Socialist Party (SSP) – abandoning Trotskyism, and the goal of building a Marxist party, in the process – the CWI in Scotland (International Socialists) are winning new members, both inside and outside the SSP. The CWI puts forward a principled Marxist programme in the SSP, and is to the forefront of the opposition to the increasingly reformist and left-nationalist policies of the SSP leadership.

The Dutch CWI, Offensief, has won members of the Socialist Party (a broad left party), by advocating Marxist ideas inside the party. In 2003, Offensief supporters, and other SP activists, managed to force the SP leaders to call a special meeting in Amsterdam to discuss the SP's limited internal democracy and the party's left reformist policies. This led to an attack on Offensief supporters by the Amsterdam SP leadership. However, in the following year, new Offensief supporters were won inside the SP, including a SP councillor, who joins other SP councillors, in the town of Breda, that support Offensief

Alternativa Socialista, in Portugal, participates in the Left Bloc and a CWI member sits on the Bloc's National Table, its national leadership body. Again, the task of Marxists in a broad formation like the Left Bloc is to promote a bold socialist programme and action that can win the support of the working class and youth.

The CWI also consistently struggles alongside local working class communities. Socialists in the Czech Republic, Socialisticka Alternativa Budoucnost (CWI), work with tenants' organisations in Prague in a fight to stop the privatisation of their homes.

A campaign against the hated bin tax, in southern Ireland, reached a peak in 2003, when local councils tried to implement the unfair levy in Dublin's working class areas. The Socialist Party (CWI) were to the fore in the mass community opposition to this tax, helping to organise demonstrations to stop the bin collectors operating. At the same time, the campaign made an appeal to council workers to join the struggle. For taking this principled stand, anti-bin tax campaigners were brought to court and some were imprisoned, including Joe Higgins, Socialist Party TD (Member of Parliament) for Dublin West, Clare Daly, who is a Socialist Party councillor in North Dublin, and other courageous youth and community activists, including Socialist Party members. By fighting in the interests of working people, Clare Daly was re-elected as a local councillor in June 2004, topping the poll, and Joe Higgins won an excellent vote, in the same month, when he stood for the European parliament.

Strengthening the CWI

Since the 'History of the CWI' was first published, in 1998, the CWI has strengthened, or even re-built sections and groups, and also implanted the CWI in new areas of the world.

One of the most impressive developments is in Belgium where, through audacious and determined campaigning work, amongst youth, in unions and in elections, the comrades have built a significant presence in both the Flemish and French speaking parts of the country. The section won 20,000 votes during the European elections in 2004. Similarly, the CWI in Sweden produces a weekly paper and is involved in all the major struggles in society, such as the council workers' strike in 2002. The section was a main force behind the anti-capitalist protests in Gothenburg in 2001, fought for women's rights, and also campaigned against the far right (facing physical attacks in the process).

The second largest CWI section, after the SP in England and Wales, is the Democratic Socialist Movement (DSM) in Nigeria. This achievement followed a significant change in the country, once the last military dictatorship fell. For years, the DSM comrades worked under military repression, winning influence and respect for their class approach amongst the poor, workers and students. Towards the end of military rule, in 1998, the DSM was launched as an open organisation. The new 'democratic' period of civilian rule saw the DSM respond with boldness and initiative, and the growth of the section was rapid after 1999. The section is an important component of the broad, radical Nigerian Conscience Party (NCP) and has authority amongst organised workers, especially in Lagos. Nigerian CWI comrades call for militant action, including properly prepared for general strikes, to resist government attacks, like fuel price rises. The section also warns against labour leaders and the NCP leaders bending to pressures from the capitalist elite – only the building of mass, independent workers' organisations, with a socialist programme, can show a way out of poverty, corruption, and divisions along tribal, ethnic and religious lines.

Also in the neo-colonial world, the United Socialist Party, in Sri Lanka, is rebuilding the rich traditions of genuine Trotskyism on the island. Unique amongst the left, the USP contains members from both the Sinhalese and Tamil sections of the population, and wins support from the wider communities during numerous elections.

The CWI in the US, Socialist Alternative, is now present in cities and towns across the continental sized country. A high priority is put on winning youth, in the universities, colleges and in the communities. Socialist Alternative participated in the fledging 'Labor Party' until it became no more than a pressure group on the big business Democrats. During the 2000 and 2004 Presidential election races, Socialist Alternative called for a vote for Ralph Nader. Despite Nader's limited radical policies, he attracts many youth and workers, looking for an alternative to the two big business parties. During Nader supporters' rallies and meetings, the CWI comrades put forward a socialist position, arguing that only this can build a viable mass alternative. Recent energetic anti-racist and anti-fascist campaigning by the CWI in Toronto is also helping to widen the influence of that group in Canada.

In some countries the political situation was relatively 'dormant' for years, but once the working class and youth were awoken, the CWI responded. The CWI in Japan participated in the large anti-war demonstrations in 2003 and put forward a socialist case against foreign military adventures in Iraq. The CWI comrades in Cyprus find a warm response to their call for working class unity and a socialist solution on the divided island. CWI supporters in Spain and the Caribbean, for example, took part in anti-government, anti-war movements in 2003/2004, and are involved in struggling to build fighting, democratic unions.

New sections

The section in Israel, Maavak Sozialisti, was officially established in 1999. It stands for workers' unity against the bosses and the Sharon government, and has given important support and assistance to workers' struggles in Israel. The Maavak Sozialisti comrades also support the right of Palestinians to self-determination, and advocate an independent, socialist Palestine, alongside a socialist Israel, as part of a socialist confederation of the region.

The CWI now also campaigns in the extremely difficult situation in Kashmir, a country divided and occupied, and which suffers terrible repression, poverty and joblessness. It is against this background that CWI members helped organise May Day demonstrations calling for workers' unity.

New CWI groups were established in New Zealand (2003), Poland (2004) and Italy (2004). Convinced that the CWI is the best Trotskyist international force, these comrades are striving to build in their countries.

The last few years have also seen a resurgence in the activities of the CWI in South Africa, the Democratic Socialist Movement (DSM). The end of apartheid was a huge step forward for the black masses, but the coming to power of the ANC government on a neo-liberal programme provoked dismay and even disillusionment amongst many on the left. These included some former CWI supporters, who concluded that globalisation and capitalism were unstoppable systems that socialists could do little to change. The CWI, however, pointed to the limits of globalisation and the need for the working class to organise to consciously change society (arguments that are increasingly accepted by growing numbers of youth and workers in South Africa and internationally). Armed with a confident programme, the DSM is re-building its forces in South Africa, and helps to lead struggles against privatisation in the townships and against fees hikes in the colleges. The bitter experience of life under pro-capitalist ANC governments means the DSM's call for a new mass workers' party is becoming more popular amongst the masses.

An important factor in the success of establishing the CWI in new parts of the world is the role of the CWI websites. The CWI's main site (socialistworld.net) and the CWI's resource and archive site (Marxist.net) are vital means of spreading Trotskyist ideas internationally. Alongside socialistworld.net (which is widely seen as one of the best left sites internationally), the sites of many national sections of the CWI are bringing fresh forces to the CWI. Clearly, Trotskyism on the internet is an invaluable compliment to the newspapers, journals, pamphlets and books of the CWI and its sections.

The CWI has also built new forces in countries where we previously were involved in necessary debates that led to some former members leaving our ranks and leaving Marxism. Following our break with the increasingly reformist leaders of the 'Labour Party Pakistan' (LPP) in 1998, the CWI re-organised as the 'United Socialist Party'. This enhanced the position of the CWI in Pakistan, especially in the eyes of many left activists who are fed up with the corruption and sell-outs of their 'leaders'. In 2003, other socialists from the revolutionary left in Pakistan joined the CWI, to form the 'Socialist Movement'. With the newly established group's influence in unions and amongst communities, allied with a correct programme and policies, the CWI is now poised to make significant headway in Pakistan.

The French CWI section, Gauche revolutionaire (GR), emerged from the debates inside the French CWI group over several years. Eventually, some former members returned to the Mandelite LCR, and quickly dissolved into the left reformist milieu. The Gauche revolutionaire comrades have, in contrast, built an important base for revolutionary Trotskyism in northern French towns, like Rouen, and in other parts of the country. The section has important points of support in the teachers' unions and amongst youth. Early in 2004, a GR member stood as part of a LCR/LO slate in local elections, putting forward the GR programme, and won a respectable vote.

Enduring and relevant ideas of Trotskyism

The fact that the CWI has not only maintained a presence in the former Soviet Union, but also extended its support across the CIS, including in Russia, Kazakhstan, the Ukraine and Moldova, and is currently winning new supporters in the Central Asian republics, is a testament to the enduring and relevant ideas of Trotskyism in the land of the 1917 socialist revolution. Conditions in the CIS ('Commonwealth of Independent States') have markedly worsened since the collapse of Stalinism and restoration of capitalism, leading to a fall in life expectancy. The working class has suffered big defeats and is mainly at the stage of re-assembling its independent organisations. However, despite these factors, and the barrage of ruling class attacks on Bolshevism and Marxism, the CWI has managed to build an important presence in the CIS. Youth, trade union and anti-war campaigns (including against the ongoing Chechen conflict), have raised the profile of the CWI and brought new working class and youth militants to its ranks. Furthermore, the CWI has had to resist the high levels of corruption and opportunism in the workers' movement, and to uphold the principled position of Marxism. No other Trotskyist force, let alone any left organisation, has managed the same success in the former Soviet Union.

In fact, no other avowedly Trotskyist organisation has the same international presence as the CWI. Of course, the CWI is still a relatively small force and the task in front of it – the socialist transformation of society - is enormous. Nevertheless, armed with the rich ideas and traditions of Marxism and Trotskyism, the CWI membership is not daunted by the road ahead. Rather, the CWI looks forward confidently to playing its part in creating mighty organisations of the working class and a new mass workers' international, which can set about ridding the world of capitalism and all its horrors, once and for all.

For more information on any of the issues mentioned above, and to follow CWI campaigns and activities, visit the CWI website:

www.socialistworld.net

Glossary

Glossary of parties and organisations

Comintern (Communist or Third International) – Founded in 1919 as world revolutionary party; under Stalin became a counter-revolutionary instrument of foreign policy and furthered the interests of the privileged ruling caste in Russia; dissolved in 1943

Committee for a Workers' International (CWI) –
International Trotskyist organisation, with affiliated organisations and parties in over 35 countries

Democracia Socialista (DS) – Brazilian section of the USFI (see below)

Fourth International – Established by Trotsky and co-thinkers in 1938 as revolutionary successor to Second and Third Internationals; however, after Trotsky's death and following WW2, the Fourth International degenerated and split, under the leadership of Mandel, Pablo, J P Cannon and co.

International Working Men's Association (First International) – Founded in 1864, with Marx and Engels as central leaders; organised many workers in Europe and North America; faced stiff repression after 1871 Paris Commune; went into decline and dissolved in 1876

International Socialists (IS) – CWI section in Scotland

International Socialist Movement (ISM) – Majority leadership grouping in Scottish Socialist Party (see below), which left the CWI in early 2001

International Socialist Tendency (IST) – International grouping established by Tony Cliff; dominated by its British section, the Socialist Workers' Party (SWP)

Liga Internacional de los Trabajadores (LIT – International Workers' League) – 'Morenite' tendency, mainly based in Latin America

Unidad Internacional de los Trabajadores (UIT – International Workers' Unity) – 1995 split from the LIT

Ligue Communiste Revolutionnaire (LCR) – USFI section in France

Linksruck – IST/SWP tendency in Germany

Lutte Ouvriere (LO) – a Trotskyist party in France

Respect Unity Coalition ('Respect') –
electoral grouping in Britain, dominated by the SWP and expelled Labour MP, George Galloway

Partito della Rifondazione Communiste (PRC) –
Left party in Italy, formed in the 1991 from a split in former Italian Communist Party

P-SOL (Party of Socialism and Liberty) – Brazilian party, which was formed in 2004 by expelled and ex-PT (Workers' Party) members, including Trotskyist groups

Scottish Socialist Party (SSP) – broad left party formed in late 1990s

United Secretariat of the Fourth International (USFI – 'Fourth International') -
International tendency which was led for a long time by Ernest Mandel

contacting the CWI

The Committee for a Workers' international (CWI) has affiliated parties and organisations in more than 35 countries, on all continents. The way to contact our comrades differs from country to country. Some you can contact directly. For others, it is easier to do so via the CWI office in London. To contact the CWI, e-mail: cwi@worldsoc.co.uk or contact us at PO Box 3688, London, Ell 1YE, Britain. Telephone: + 44 (0)20 8988 8760. Fax: + 44 (0)20 8988 8793. Visit our website at: http://www.socialistworld.net If you want to know more about the CWI in Cyprus, Finland, Ghana, Kashmir, Luxembourg, Pakistan, Poland, Spain or anywhere else... then contact the CWI international offices above.

Australia: Socialist Party
PO Box 1015, Collingwood, Victoria 3066
phone: + 61 3 9650 0160 e-mail: sp@mira.net
Austria: Sozialistische Linkspartei
Kaiserstrasse 14/11, 1070 Wien phone: + 43 1
524 6310 fax: + 43 1 524 6311 e-mail: slp@slp.at
Belgium: LSP/MAS PO Box 10, 1190 Vorst 3,
phone: + 32 2 345 6181
e-mail: lspmas@skynet.be
Brazil: Socialismo Revolucionario Caixa Postal
02009, CEP 01 060-970, Sao Paulo S.P.
phone: + 55 11 339 5584
e-mail: sr-cio@uol.com.br
Canada: Socialist Alternative
903-633 Bay Street, Toronto, Ontario MSG 2G4
e-mail: socialist@ canada.com
Chile: Socialismo Revolucionario
Celso C Campos, Cassilla 50310, Correo
Central, Santiago phone: + 56 2 622 9004
e-mail: jandresvena@hotmail.com
CIS 125167 Moscow a\Ya 37, Moscow, Russia
e-mail: pabgem@online.ru
Czech Republic: Socialistická Alternativa
Budoucnost D.V.S., PO Box 227, Bubesnké
nábfieêi 306, 170 05 Praha 7 - Hole_ovice
e-mail: budoucnost@email.cz
England & Wales: Socialist Party PO Box 24697,
London E11 1YD phone: + 44 20 8988 8777
fax: + 44 20 8988 8787
e-mail: campaigns@socialistparty.org.uk
France: Gauche révolutionnaire Les amis de
l'Egalite Centre 166, 82 rue Jeanne d' Arc,
76000 Rouen e-mail: grcontact@hotmail.com
Germany: Sozialistische Alternative
Litten Strasse 106/107, 10179 Berlin
phone: + 49 30 2472 3802
e-mail: info@sav-online.de
Greece: Xekinima 8 Gortynos Street, PO Box
11254, Athens phone/fax: + 30 210 228 3018
e-mail: xekinima@hotmail.com
India: Dudiyora Horaata
PO Box 1828, Bangalore 560018
e-mail: dudiyorahoraata@vsnl.net

Ireland North: Socialist Party
15 Lombard Street, Belfast BT1 1RB
phone: + 44 2890 232962
fax: + 44 2890 311778
e-mail: socialist@belfastsp.freeserve.co.uk
Ireland South: Socialist Party PO Box 3434,
Dublin 8 phone/fax: + 353 1 677 25 92
e-mail: info@socialistparty.net
Israel: Maavak Sozialisti
P.O.B. 4102, Jaffa e-mail: info@maavak.org.il
Italy: Lotta per il Socialismo
e-mail: lottaperilsoc@hotmail.com
Japan: Kokusai Rentai Kanayamachi Biru 3F
Kita-ku, Temma 2-1-17, Osaka-shi 530-0043
e-mail: kokusairentai@hotmail.com
Netherlands: Offensief PO Box 11561, 1001 GN
Amsterdam e-mail: info@offensief.nl
New Zealand: Socialist Alternative
e-mail: socialist_alternative@hotmail.com
Nigeria: Democratic Socialist Movement
PO Box 2225, Agege, Lagos
phone: +234 1 804 6603
e-mail: dsmcentre@hotmail.com
Portugal: Alternativa Socialista
Apartado 27018, 1201-950, Lisboa
e-mail: Alternativa_socialista@clix.pt
Scotland: International Socialists PO Box 6773,
Dundee DD1 IYL phone: + 44 1382 833 759
e-mail: cwi@blueyonder.co.uk
South Africa: Democratic Socialist Movement
PO Box 596, Newton, 2113 Johannesburg
phone: + 27 11 342 2220
e-mail: democraticsocialist@mweb.co.za
Sri Lanka: United Socialist Party
261/1 Kirula Road, Narahenpito, Colombo 5
phone: + 94 1 508 821 e-mail: usp@wow.lk
Sweden: Rattvisepartiet Socialisterna
PO Box 73, 123 03 Farsta
phone: + 46 8 605 9400 fax: + 46 8 556 252 52
e-mail: rs@socialisterna.org
USA: Socialist Alternative
PO Box 45343, Seattle W4 98145
e-mail: info@socialistalternative.org